Political

Perspectives

A Poetry Collection

MARIO PANAYI

Acknowledgements

A huge thank you to Stuart Inston and Jeremy Jeavons for encouraging me to write this collection.

Stuart suggested a satirical poem on Enoch Powell and the Rivers of Blood speech. I explained that I could not justify a satirical piece of poetry on an issue so contentious and explosive, but that I would write a non-satirical poem on what he suggested instead.

Jeremy, on the other hand, was eager for me to write a poem on Theresa May's dancing capabilities.

Contents

Foreword

Politics is ruthless. It divides friends and family. Heated arguments can occur as different opinions flare up. Careers and reputations can be destroyed in a spectacular manner. Often capabilities of politicians are eclipsed by their own personal and private lives being exposed.

To be a politician, you need to be tough. The rewards can be huge. The scandals and criticism they receive can be even greater. Their friends and relatives are also under the microscope. As for anyone having a secret affair, those secrets and affairs are like food to those reporting political news who are determined to cut through and digest the juiciest revelations and not leave any morsel behind.

The views expressed in this poetry collection are not the views of the author but instead a look at the rollercoaster rides that some of the politicians and their loved ones have experienced. This includes the varying opinions expressed in traditional mainstream media and social media.

Politics

A cocktail with a lethal

And potent mix of ingredients

More dangerous and longer lasting

Than world wars and *Game of Thrones*

An ensemble cast

Larger than every soap opera ever made

Politicians are criticised and ridiculed daily

We cringe at their antics and their words

We are Judge, Jury and Executioners

Cruelly and gruesomely dissecting every decision

And every part of their character

Luckily for us, the viewers

Of the longest ongoing soap opera in history

Is that the cast provides us with the ammunition

As we uncover their lies, deceit and corruption

Boreas

In Greek mythology
There was an ancient God
Of the North winds
His name was Boreas

He was full of bluster
Blowing harsh winds
Even overturning
Army fleets on the seas

He was also a God of winter
Filling the lands with ice
With cold air that he breathed
A coldness that replicated his soul

There were even stories
That he would transform
Into a winged horse to ravish mares
And from those mares he sired offspring

Lovers he amassed
His wife Orithyia bore him four children

He fathered Butes by an unknown woman

And Pitys was his frequent mistress

His description has survived

In classical texts

Shaggy and wild hair

With his bloated face full of wind

Now there are also legends

That his descendants still live

Echoing his physique

And womanising ways

There is one descendant in particular

That has surpassed his ancestor, Boreas

Taking and modernising his name

But still full of bluster as he huffs and puffs

Cleopatra

Pharaoh

Politician

Seductress

Immortalised eternally

In film, art and books

Legendary forever

Even her name

Conjures up

Her fame and reputation

The Ides of March

Beware the Ides of March

The Ides of March are come

Aye, Caesar, but not gone

Assassinated by 60 senators

Led by his so-called friend

Et tu, Brutus?

Who many say was his actual son

His legacy continues

Political accomplishments

And warrior conquests

But his name gave rise

To the terms;

Tsar and Kaiser

And even the word caesarean

Ultimately,

The assassination

Of Julius Caesar

Showcases how enemies conspire

Ruthless and even capable of murder

In order to save their own power

Religion and Politics

Religion and politics

Are a lethal combination

They are like oil and water

Or two chemicals which

When combined

Cause an explosion

There are many examples

Of religious figures

Who influenced politics

Resulting in encountering hardships

Assassination attempts

And sometimes even a gruesome death;

Cardinal Thomas Wolsey

Mahatma Gandhi

Archbishop Makarios III

Ian Paisley

Yet despite their explosive nature

When combined together

Every now and then

Religious figures will still step forward

Offering their opinions and guidance

On political matters

Do they belong together?

Time will tell when historians

Dissect and make their judgements

Political Crisis of Royal Proportions

There are certain political crises

That involve the monarchy

Which if not handled correctly

Could even cause anarchy

When it became clear that

Edward VI was unlikely to survive his latest illness

Politicians, archbishops, bishops, councillors,

Peers and sheriffs became involved

In making Lady Jane Grey his successor

Lady Jane Grey

Became known as

The Nine Days' Queen

As politicians yet again

Involved themselves in

Influencing who the monarch should be

Rising to the throne was Queen Mary

Who would earn the nickname Bloody Mary

On account of the volume of Protestants

She had burned at the stake

In 1763 the Member of Parliament, John Wilkes

Spread rumours that King George III's mother

Princess Dowager, formerly Princess Augusta

Was having an affair with John Stuart, the Earl of Bute

And that was the real reason that George III

Had promoted John Stuart to Prime Minister

A little hypocritical as the accuser

Was infamous for his many affairs

Including with prostitutes

And he was removed from Parliament the following year

Due to his alleged published pornographic writings

In 1799, *The Grand Old Duke of York*

He had 10,000 men

He marched them up to the top of the hill

And he marched them down again

And when they were up, they were up

And when they were down, they were down

And when they were only halfway up

They were neither up nor down

But the real downfall of Prince Frederick, Duke of York

Was ten years later in 1809

When a scandal broke regarding his mistress

Mary Anne Clarke who had been accused

Of selling army commissions with the Duke's knowledge

To furnish their lavish lifestyle

It was a House of Commons Select Committee

That investigated the various accusations against the Duke

Resulting in the Duke's resignation

George IV had run up many debts

Parliament agreed to pay off his debts

So long as he married Princess Caroline of Brunswick

The agreement was carried out

But the marriage was full of hatred

George IV was determined

That his wife would never be queen

And that he obtain a divorce

The matter went to the House of Lords

But the attempt to divorce Caroline

Proved to be unpopular with the British people

As George IV tried to provide evidence

That she was an adulterer

When he himself had several mistresses

And was infamous for his immoral behaviour

The attempt to obtain a divorce

Through the House of Lords

Was too hypocritical to gain any merit

When Edward VIII

Declared his love for Wallis Simpson

And his intention to marry her

After her second divorce was finalised

Yet again politicians involved themselves

In the monarchy

The opposition to the relationship

Resulted in the abdication of Edward VIII

He married his lover Wallis

And it turned out to be *third time lucky*

For Wallis remained married to Edward

Until his death thirty-five years later

The intertwined relationship

Between politicians and the monarchy

Remain to this day

Particularly the relationship

Of the Prime Minster and the Monarch

Portrayed in television series such as *The Crown*

Commented upon in the newspapers and the internet

And shown live in televised debates and proceedings

"Surely the Prime Minister can have the humility

To say sorry – for misleading the Queen

Misleading the country and illegally

Shutting down our democracy"

5th of November

Remember, remember

The fifth of November

In the year Sixteen oh Five

When gunpowder traitors were caught alive

They were sentenced

Hung, drawn and quartered

Part of British political history

Their fame remaining a mystery

Penny for the Guy

Fireworks that fly

Bonfires alight

All through the night

Stable

There once was a soon-to-be MP who was quite unstable

In the middle of the night he literally went to the stables

Then woke up the hosts of Woburn Abbey at 5.00 am

A Duke and Duchess whilst in their bed

He was covered in blood and presented them

With several severed ears from horses' heads

And although this sounds like some wild tale

Sorry to disappoint, it's true, every single detail

His name was Robert Carteret

But he's now dead, so try not to fret

The Hurling of Insults

Although members of parliament
Are meant to represent their constituents
And have strict code of ethics
When riled their vocabulary
Becomes scathing to the extreme

"The insignificant little fellow in the wig."
"You're a miserable pipsqueak of a man, Gove."
"The House has noticed the Prime Minister's
Remarkable transformation in the last few weeks
From Stalin to Mr Bean."
"He's like a shiver looking for a spine to run up."
"More of a ventriloquist's dummy than a Prime Minister."
"Is Boris a very, very clever man pretending to be an
idiot?"
… Nicola Sturgeon is *"Lady McBeth."*
But Nicola herself makes brash and bold remarks,
As she suggests she ought to buy Boris Johnson *"a*
hairbrush."

Whatever century or country you look at
The insults are there

Hurled with pride

And with self-admiration

Rasputin of Russia

A figure whose life and death

Was embroiled in mystery and speculation

A mystic? A religious man? A charlatan?

An influencer on the Tsar and Tsarina

And hence on the politics of Russia

The influence Rasputin had

Led to him becoming a hated figure

A man who was so hated

That murder attempts on his life began

Until actually murdered

Stabbed and survived

Poisoned and he asked for wine

Poisoned again and still alive

Shot and believed to have died

Until he leapt and fought his way to freedom

Once outside he was shot again

Finally murdered and his body

Thrown into a river

The murderers included

Noblemen and a politician

Years later rumours surfaced

Of Rasputin's penis having been severed

Worshipped by those who were infertile

Now on display in a museum in St Petersburg

Which beggars the question, who's the real cock?

Anastasia

Although not a politician

She was the youngest daughter

Of the last Tsar and Tsarina of Russia

Murdered along with her entire family

In a shower of bullets

On the orders of those who sought political power

The assassination of Nicholas II and his family

And others murdered via revolutions

Including Nicolae and Elena Ceausescu,

Saddam Hussein and Colonel Gaddafi

Showcases that those who have taken the political power

Are determined to ensure that their predecessor

And their descendants have no way back

Hence why they order a permanent gruesome solution

Anastasia stayed true to the meaning of her name

As sightings of the young Anastasia

Whose name means *resurrection*

Continued for decades

Showing the power and strength

That exists in those named Anastasia

Emmeline and Emily

Women's suffrage;
The right to vote
Was valiantly fought
With words and demonstrations
Violence and prison sentences

Brave women
That were determined
To obtain the right to vote
Even through illegal tactics
Fierce and fuelled with passion

Emmeline Pankhurst
For years at the forefront
Of organising and progressing
The suffragette movement
Including by militant means

Emily Wilding Davison
Dedicated her life and death
To fighting for women's suffrage
Culminating in being trampled
By King George V's horse, Anmer

In their time they were considered

Militant criminals who were often arrested

Enduring hunger strikes and imprisonment

Now considered pioneers and martyred

With statues and plaques, in film and even song

Laurence Housman

Using his artistic talents

He progressed political issues

Including the suffrage movement

To give women the right to vote

To de-stigmatise homosexuality

To promote equality

Often by highlighting

Inequalities and injustices

Through satire, humour

And thought-provoking eloquent art

Nancy Astor

In November 1919 Nancy Astor

Became the first woman to sit

As a member of parliament

In the House of Commons

And remained in office

Until her resignation

Over twenty-five years later

It is her relationship with the future Prime Minister

Winston Churchill that created humorous exchanges

When Churchill allegedly said

That having a woman in parliament is like

Having someone intrude on him in the bathroom

She apparently replied,

"You're not handsome enough to have such fears."

When Churchill asked what disguise he should wear

To a masquerade ball, Lady Astor is said to have replied,

"Why don't you come sober, Prime Minister?"

In another exchange of words

Lady Astor is purported to have said,

"Oh, if you were my husband, I'd put poison in your tea."

To which Winston Churchill is meant to have replied,

"If I were your husband, I'd drink it with pleasure."

One hundred years after her election to parliament

A bronze statue of Nancy Astor was erected

Perhaps showcasing that becoming the first female

Sitting Member of Parliament in the House of Commons

Paved the way to a future prime minister dubbed The Iron

Lady

Keep it in the Family – Part 1

The Member of Parliament Robert Boothby

From 1930 onwards had an affair

With Lady Dorothy Macmillan

Who just happened to be the wife

Of future Prime Minister, Harold MacMillan

There were even rumours that Boothby

Had fathered her youngest child

When Lady Dorothy's brother died

And suspicion fell on whether *the doctor did it*

A thorough investigation was not made

In order not to draw attention

To the affair of Robert and Dorothy

Robert later married Diana Cavendish

Who just happened to be

Lady Dorothy's first cousin

The second cousin of Robert Boothby

Whose name was Sir Ludovic Kennedy

Suggested that Robert had fathered

At least three children by the wives of other men

Winston

With his famous cigar-gravelled voice
His words shaped politics and philosophy

"Politics is more dangerous than war,
For in war you are only killed once."

"I may be drunk, Miss, but in the morning
I will be sober and you will still be ugly."

"A lie gets halfway around the world,
Before the truth has a chance to get its pants on."

Wife. Widow. Woman.

She was known as the First Lady

Wife of President John F. Kennedy

Spending more money on fashion accessories

Classy and elegant clothes and jewellery

Than her husband's salary as the President

She was next to her husband

When he was assassinated

The dramatic and devastating scenes

Seen by the entire world

Now entering her widowhood period

Ultimately, Jackie Bouvier Kennedy

Was an extraordinary woman

Discarding the black clothes and mourning

Fulfilling her womanly desires

With a new marriage and an extravagant lifestyle

Conquering the world

As a woman

As the wife of the President of America

As a widow whose mourning was watched by all

And as the ultimate survivor of tragedy

Redemption

John Profumo

Achieved much in his life

But his achievements

Are usually overshadowed

By his affair with the young

And attractive, Christine Keller

He accomplished much in the army

Rising to Brigadier and awarded medals

For his bravery and distinguished accomplishments

In parliament he again displayed integrity

Despite David Margesson's outburst

In which he told John, *"I can tell you this,*

You utterly contemptible little shit.

On every morning that you wake up

For the rest of your life you will be ashamed

Of what you did last night."

It is almost as though Margesson

Cursed John Profumo

Because it was John's subsequent affair

With Christine Keller that haunted him

For decades after the affair had ended

Although at the time

John Profumo was demonised

Disgraced and humiliated

Resigned in the midst of a media frenzy

John Profumo dedicated the remainder

Of his long life to raising the profile

And donations for charity

He was a cliché example of *hero to zero*

But ultimately he was hard-working

Dedicated to promoting good

And had he not fallen from grace

In a time where extra-marital affairs

Were considered virtually evil

Perhaps he would have continued

His rise in politics and who knows

If he had lived in a different era

Or had not succumbed to a lustful affair

He could even have become Prime Minister

Harold Wilson

He became Prime Minister

Of the United Kingdom twice

From 1964 to 1970, and again

1974 to 1976 and his accomplishments

For that time were modern and radical

He abolished capital punishment –

No more threat of the death penalty

Theatre censorship was also abolished

Homosexuality was decriminalised

Divorce laws were relaxed making it

Less complicated and difficult to divorce

Abortion laws were also relaxed

Giving pregnant women more choice

Corporal punishment ended in schools

And he oversaw the referendum

Which led to Great Britain joining

The European Economic Community

Which would later become known as

The European Union

So many things that people these days

Take for granted, were the result

Of Harold Wilson's premiership

Modernising and relaxing

Stern, authoritative and dictatorial measures

Of people's basic human rights

To love, legally divorce and live

Rivers of Blood

Over 2,040 years ago

Virgil wrote *The Aeneid*

Where he famously stated a prophecy that

"… wars, terrible wars …" would lead to

"The Tiber foaming with much blood."

Almost 2,000 years later

Enoch Powell makes his infamous

Rivers of Blood speech

A speech that divided a nation

Where racism was at the core of the speech

Throughout the last 2,000 years

And no doubt throughout the next 2,000

Wars, racism and discrimination will soar

History repeating itself

Over and over again

The terms might change

From *The Tiber foaming with much blood*

The Rivers of Blood speech

To *Black Lives Matter*

But the divide remains

The blood of white

Of black and every race

Continues to run like rivers

Floating into an ocean

Of death and mourning

And there is no distinction

In the colour of their blood

As that blood soaks together

Fused finally without fear or anger

Instead a melancholic deep, deep red

Did Dead MP Tell Tales?

Your political career

Can die more than once

And resurrect itself

But one MP decided

To fake his own death

He was soon discovered

To still be alive

Living in Australia

Under a different name

Twelve years later

He actually died

Proving that

You Only Live Twice

The MP, the Blackmailer, an Assassin and a Dog

A tale so incredible

That not only did it make

Front page news

But decades later made

Into a television mini-series

An MP who had allegedly

Had a gay affair or one-night stand

In an age when homosexuality was illegal

Which then resulted in several years

Of one of the most bizarre associations ever

The alleged lover of the MP Jeremy Thorpe

Was Norman Josiffe, AKA Norman Scott

Who over the years resorted to various tactics

Including syphoning sympathy and money

And emotional blackmail turning into actual blackmail

Norman made various allegations

To whoever would listen

He went to the press

Instigated political investigations

And spiralled into wrath, depression and bitterness

Jeremy contemplated various methods

To silence the hindrance to his reputation and career

What happens next involves a gunman, a Great Dane and
  Norman

Rinka the dog is assassinated, more allegations, and trials

A tale of a friendship where gratitude turns into resentment

Winter of Discontent

From 14 degrees

It dropped overnight

To zero degrees

Echoing the mood

Of the nation

Bitterly cold

As the strikes

And discontent

Continued to slide

Just like the icy weather

Lorry drivers went on strike

Unions clashed with Government

Newspapers ridiculed the Prime Minister

With the headlines, *'Crisis, What crisis?'*

Jim Callaghan was photographed

In Barbados in his bathing suit

And swimming in the sea

Rail workers, nurses,

Public sector, private sector

The discontent continued to rise

As the winter created havoc

One strike referred to as *Misery Monday*

Strike action increased intensely

Grave diggers striked for the first time ever

Waste disposal workers joined in

The repercussions were *grave*

As stored bodies waiting for burial

Increased to the point that even

Burial at sea was considered by one council

No rubbish collections resulted

In increased rat infestation and activity

Leicester Square being nicknamed *Fester Square*

Ultimately, there were over

Two thousand strikes

In the winter of 1978 to 1979

And Shakespeare's words

The winter of our discontent

Were certainly a true depiction

Of the misery and torment

That existed and manifested

In people uniting together

Against Government policy

The Incredible Sulk

After resigning his position

As Leader of the Conservative Party

His ambivalence towards his successor

And other personality traits he exhibited

Resulted in the press dubbing him

As *The Incredible Sulk*

Ted was offered by Margaret

Any position he wanted

On her Shadow Cabinet

But he rebuffed her offer

Margaret as a gracious winner

Visited the man who would become

One of her greatest critics

Again she offered Ted

Whatever position he wanted

And also for him to lead the campaign

To join the European Union

Again Ted refused

To try and reduce the impact

Of how short her visit to Ted Heath was

Margaret stayed for coffee

With Ted's personal private secretary

Ted's entire reaction

Following the leadership contest

Of the Conservative Party

Is just one example of why the media

Referred to Ted as *The Incredible Sulk*

Margaret

She changed the world forever
The first female Prime Minister
Of the United Kingdom
Dubbed The Iron Lady
Because of her unbreakable will
Determined to push through her policies
Dividing the country
With her legacy of change

Thatcher the Milk Snatcher
The Falklands War
The Miners' Strike
The Right to Buy
Privatisation
The Poll Tax

Showcasing her dry wit with words
"The Lady's not for turning."
"A week is a long time in politics."
"It may be the cock that crows,
But it is the hen that lays the eggs."

Gone but never forgotten
Part of world history
Margaret Thatcher

What Her Allies and Rivals Said About Her

Maggie Thatcher divided Great Britain
Europe and the entire world
Resulting in many comments about her;

Do you dress as a leader, a woman,
for yourself, or for your husband?

It's been a touching spectacle;
The brave little woman
getting on with the woman's work
of trying to dominate the world

In her presence you quickly forget she's a woman.
She doesn't strike me as a very female type

What does she want, this housewife?
My balls on a tray?

The Iron Man

Attila the Hen

She has the eyes of Caligula

But the mouth of Marilyn Monroe

My God, the bitch has won

Shrill and hectoring

Coal, not dole

Ditch the bitch

Had Margaret Thatcher been a man
The derogatory and demeaning comments
About being a *housewife* and about her *femininity*
Would never, ever have been made
And yet, she rose above all those comments
For she could give as good as she got

But as a nation and the wider world
Has sex discrimination reduced?
Or has it just become more covert?
More well-hidden than before

Savaged by a Dead Sheep

A mild mannered gentleman

Thick, silvery and wavy hair

Akin to a sheep's clotted coat of wool

Described by a colleague

That any verbal exchange with Geoffrey

Was *"Like being savaged by a dead sheep."*

Yet his resignation speech

Whilst long and monotoned

Delivered the beginning of the end

Of the Thatcher era

He was not a wolf in sheep's clothing

But a sheep amongst wolves

Who stopped bleating

Standing tall in the middle of the flock

He learnt to roar like a lion

Tarzan

With his tall, thin, athletic build
And windswept, unkempt hair
Tarzan entered into a new jungle
No longer swinging through trees
And a friend to all species of animals

Instead he ducked, dived and punched
Taking on one beast after another
With eloquent speeches and charisma
Becoming more confident and determined
With each fierce and feral battle

He even took on and toppled
A mythical beast known as The Iron Lady
Perhaps a descent of the bronze giant Talon
But Tarzan never became King of this new Jungle
Never achieved cohesion amongst the beasts
Instead sulkily left and retired

But every now and then
He would swing back into action
His distinct echo call heard loud and clear
As he still tried to champion
His own brand of politics to the jungle

What Goes Around, Comes Around

When Margaret Thatcher

Was ousted as Prime Minister

And Leader of the Conservative Party

In a similar fashion to her predecessor

Ted Heath was asked in an interview

If it was true that he reacted

By saying, *"Rejoice, Rejoice."*

Ted Heath humorously replied,

"I think I said it three times."

Tony Benn

If ever there was a Champion
Of the working-class men and women
It was the politician Tony Benn
Eloquent, principled and direct
With thought-provoking speeches
Intuitive, interesting and informative

If ever there was a Champion
Of anti-war campaigns
It was the politician Tony Benn
Who was also a Champion
Against different forms of discrimination;
Including women's rights, gay rights, and race relations
Yet again, Tony Benn was there

He was never the Leader of a political party
But always leading by example
He fought for his beliefs
Debating with wise words
Truly a man before his time

Perhaps his only real folly
Being his trademark pipe

A Purge on Perjury

You would expect

That politicians would adhere

To certain basic moral and ethical standards

Adhere to the laws which they themselves influence

Honesty being an admirable quality to possess

Yet case after case politicians gives themselves

A bad, bad reputation of bending the truth

And even lying under oath

Jeffrey Archer was one such politician

Who lied under oath in a libel case

About whom he had being lying in bed with

He was awarded compensation

But the truth of his perjury soon came out

He had indeed paid a prostitute money

Resulting in the end of his political career

And a four-year stint in prison for perjury

In 1995 a *World in Action* programme

About Jonathan Aitken and an alleged

Arms deal and link with the Saudi Royal Family

Was broadcast entitled, *Jonathan of Arabia*

Jonathan then sued for libel

But further investigation revealed

The full scope of his perjury

Resulting in an eighteen month prison sentence

Fast forward several years

Jonathan Aitken was ordained

Ironically he now serves as a chaplain

in Her Majesty's Pentonville Prison

"I did not have sexual liaisons

With that woman, Ms. Lewinsky."

Only President Bill Clinton

Did indeed have sexual liaisons

His stale *seed* on her blue dress

Leading to an international media frenzy

As the President of the United States of America

Was charged with perjury and an impeachment trial

Chris Huhne was a member of the Cabinet

He denied that he had lied

About a past speeding charge

And he also denied

That someone else had accepted

The penalty points on his behalf

In order for Chris not to lose his driving license

After months of interviewing both Chris Huhne

And his ex-wife Vicky Pryce, who made the original

allegation

They were found guilty and sentenced to eight months each

Huhne and Pryce paying the ultimate *price* for perjury

And perverting the course of justice

Eggs

Politicians certainly seem

To have a fascination with eggs

The two most famous stories

Being that of Edwina Currie

And Labour's former Deputy Prime Minister

John Prescott

Edwina Currie's *salmonella in eggs scandal*

Lasted for days, weeks and months

Forced to resign but later revealed

That she had in fact spoken the truth

But the revelation of her four-year affair

With John Major was an even bigger **egg-citing** scandal

Various politicians have had eggs

And even milkshakes thrown at them

But it was John Prescott's reaction

That made the biggest headlines

As the former boxer instinctively

And dramatically punched his assailant

Silent Man of Politics

Silence can be golden

A silent assassin

Silent tears

Silent but deadly

There is a Quiet man of politics

His name is Iain Duncan Smith

A former army officer and a former Leader

Of the Conservative Party

Once dethroned as the Party Leader

The silent man slowly roared

Showcasing his real attributes

As a potentially deadly assassin

Whilst in the midst of austerity measures he authorised

£8.45 million for a mascot called *Workie*

He brought forward a rise in the pension age, and

In April 2013 he said that you could live on £53.00 per

week

The silent man of politics

Has been anything but golden

Instead arguably a deadly and silent assassin

Causing suffering and silent tears galore

Nelson Mandela

A name and man

Synonymous

With anti-racism

Anti-colonialism

Pro-democracy

Imprisoned in body

But never in his mind or his spirit

Eventually becoming a symbol of freedom

His soothing voice instantly recognisable

A political giant across the entire world

Eternally revered, respected and remembered

Winnie Mandela

A spirited woman

Who showcased to the world

The best that Heaven had to offer

And the worst that Hell on earth offered

Once known as *The Queen of Africa*

And also *The Mother of the Nation*

Yet despite her fight against apartheid

She succumbed to temptations galore

Embroiled in fraud, corruption and even murder

Her life was a gateway to imprisonment and freedom

Violence followed and caressed her from an early age

A fighter whose fists and words were her weapons of

choice

Even in the lead- up to her funeral

Critics and supporters clashed with words;

"Sit down and shut up", "Anyone who accuses

Mama Winnie of any crime is guilty of treason"

Ultimately, she represented elegance and wealth

But also poverty, desperation and ill health

Despite being violently bashed and beaten

Her spirit never waned and remained strong

But also poverty, desperation and ill health

Wives of Robert Mugabe

The first wife of Robert Mugabe
Stated, *"Talk to your pillow*
If you have problems in your marriage.
Never, ever humiliate your husband."
Mugabe referred to his wife as *Amai*
Meaning *Mother of the Nation*

After the death of wife number one
Mugabe married his long-term mistress
Who gained a reputation of spending money;
Jewellery, clothes and other expensive items
Earning herself the nickname *Gucci Grace*
But it was her violence and GBH reputation
That gave rise to her other title of *Dis-Grace*

Official Monster Raving Loony Party

Despite their party name

Never winning one election

And always losing their parliamentary deposit

Some of their manifesto pledges

Have been taken and made into law

Including, *Passports for pets*

Abolition of dog licences

And all-day pub openings

So perhaps despite their appearances

Their obvious satirical take on 'the serious nature of

politics'

They should in fact be taken seriously

As they are highlighting issues

You never know

Their policy on producing

A 99 pence coin

Might be adopted next

Lord Above

Originally, a revered reference to God

And to the son of God, Jesus Christ

Our Lady of Lourdes

Where pilgrimages are made

For prayer, faith and healing

The meaning also extending

To noblemen and male peers

A Lord in the House of Lords

The reverence aspect diminishes

With the scandal of Lord Lambton

A playboy Member of Parliament

Who was caught smoking cannabis

In a threesome with two prostitutes

His antics of regularly visiting prostitutes

Exposed in the newspapers

His defence in an interview was that

"... people like variety..... it's as simple as that..."

The dignified aspect of Lords

Is further withered down

With the arrival

Of Screaming Lord Sutch

And Lord Buckethead

The Colour Purple

In ancient times

The colour purple

Was reserved for royalty

And the elite

It gave rise to phrases like

Born in purple

Tyrian purple

The purple dyes

In those ancient times

Was expensive to produce

Including from rare sea snails

And in some cultures

The common people

Were forbidden to wear

The colour purple

Under penalty of death

The colour purple

Is also the colour

Of a sad and bruised heart

It is an unhealthy hue

As though punched

Beaten beyond repair

Weak and dying

No longer pumping

Then death arrives

And your beige body

Slowly decays

Into the deathly shade

Of Livor Mortis

The colour purple

Being adopted by UKIP

Their main party leader

Absorbing the entire history

Of the colour purple

A rich man with a common tongue

Wearing the colour of Roman Emperors

A party embroiled in physical attacks

Punches causing shades of purple bruises

The party rising and then falling

Just like the history and lifespan of all empires

And as the last gasps of UKIP breathed

The tragic and deathly colour of livor mortis

You have to ask if the pompous former leader

Now fully exposed including his rich financial backers

Is not actually a Roman Emperor in a purple tunic

But an example of the sluggish sea snails

Whose mucus was used to produce purple dye

Or perhaps a modern-day emperor without any clothes

American Scandals

Whilst the UK have had numerous political scandals

The USA have had more than their fair share of scandals

Including infamous presidential scandals

Former President Nixon; *"I am not a crook"*

Only the Watergate scandal proved otherwise

Former President Bill Clinton;

"I did not have sexual relations with that woman."

Only the dress with his stale sperm certainly did prove

That he had sexual relations with Monica Lewinsky

Devoted Wives

There are wives whose actions

Make them famous and legendary

When President Ronald Reagan first started

To exhibit symptoms of Alzheimer's disease in public

But it had yet to be revealed to the world

It was his devoted wife, First Lady Nancy Reagan

Who stood dutifully by his side

Prompting her husband with words

Reminding him where he was with his speeches

Yet when the media criticised Nancy

She silently took the media critique

In order to shield and protect her husband

On 26th January 1992 Hillary Clinton

Defended her husband

Amidst speculation on his alleged infidelities

She famously stated that *"I'm not sitting here,*

Some little woman standing by my man

Like Tammy Wynette"

Creating a feud between herself

And the country singing legend

But the most charismatic defence of a husband

Came when Rupert Murdoch

Was being grilled by a parliamentary committee

A protestor entered the proceedings

With a cream pie on a paper plate

Determined to *pie-face* the Media Mogul

Everyone was paralysed

As though watching in slow motion

Everyone except the devoted wife

As Wendi Deng sprang into action

Virtually leaping across and punching the assailant

The video clip then went viral

Making Wendi an internet sensation

But despite the enigmatic and enthusiastic actions

It was not enough to save her marriage a few years later

Amidst accusations of an affair and Chinese intelligence

Mistresses

The mistresses of politicians

Wield real power

As the knowledge of their affairs

Can destroy marriages and political careers

Even bring down a president

They can be charming and enigmatic

Intelligent or naïve

But never, ever boring

Marilyn Monroe

Arguably the most famous blonde bombshell

In the history of the entire world

Speculation and rumours circulated for years

Did she and JFK have an affair?

Was she murdered by the Kennedys?

Will the real truth ever be known?

Christine Keeler's affair with John Profumo

Became a national scandal known as

'The Profumo Affair'

An uneducated showgirl and model

A teenager who amassed lovers

Accusations galore followed

An abortion, an attack, a trial,

Perjury and imprisonment

A naïve victim?

A scapegoat?

A survivor?

Sara Keays was the personal secretary

Of the Secretary of State for Trade and Industry

The revelation of their twelve-year affair

And the fact that she was pregnant with his child

Was the downfall of both of them

Cecil Parkinson returned to parliamentary prominence

But never entered into his daughter's life

A little ironic how politicians can influences laws

Including laws based on human decency, ethics and morality

But be incapable of showing any affection

To a child that he himself fathered

Edwina Currie

Cashing in on her affair

By writing her book, *Currie's Diaries*

Revealing she'd had a four-year affair

With a former prime minster

Her remarks in recent years

Concerning her former lover

Arguably defines the phrase

A woman scorned

Whereas Edwina Currie's name

After the revelation of her affair

Was the talk of the United Kingdom

It was the revelation of Bill Clinton's affair

With a White House Intern

That made the name Monica Lewinsky

Into an international household name

She kept a semen-stained blue dress

As evidence which brought down a president

Impeachment proceedings followed

Salacious, saucy, sensational stories

Real lives with real consequences

Yet, can you imagine how many more affairs?

How many more mistresses?

Are so good at concealing their liaisons

Hidden, secret, daring and lustful

Which is their own personal business

As to the actual volume of affairs

New Labour

New Labour; A defining
And monumental political slogan
Just like the World War II slogans
Loose lips sink ships
And *Keep Calm*

Yet was New Labour new?
Or still very much red wine
In new bottles with new labels
Alternatively, did Labour abandon
Working people's values?

Blair's Babes

After the victory

Of the Labour Party

In the 1997 General Election

The new Prime Minister

Tony Blair was photographed

With his 101 new female

Members of Parliament

They were nicknamed

Blair's Babes

But was the term

Blair's Babes flattering?

Or an example of misogyny?

Keys to Number Ten

The keys to Number Ten

Arguably the most powerful house

In the whole of the United Kingdom

Rattled above the head of Tony Blair

Who was the current Prime Minister

By the resident of Number Eleven

The Chancellor Gordon Brown

Was Gordon goading and harassing Tony?

Trying to persuade him to resign

As per their alleged agreement

Known as the *Blair-Brown Deal*

A tactic and event

Chronicled in the autobiography

And interviews of Cherie Blair

Children Should Be Seen and Not Heard

It might be one of the oldest clichés

That *children should be seen but not heard*

And in political circles that certainly seems the case

On the 16th of May 1990 at the height of the BSE scare

The Agriculture Secretary John Selwyn Gummer

Tried to reassure the public that eating beef

Was not a health issue as he was quite prepared

To feed his four-year-old daughter a beef burger

Captured on video by the national press

Unfortunately, little Cordelia recoiled at the burger

She was a child that *could be seen and heard*

Amongst the *herd* of cows

Resulting in John eating the burger himself

On 5th of July 2000 a sixteen-year-old boy

Was found inebriated and vomiting

He was taken to a police station

The boy gave a false name and an old address

For his father just happened to have given a speech

A few days earlier that *on the spot fines*

Should be given to those who were

Drunk and disorderly in their behaviour

The sixteen-year-old was in fact Euan Blair

Son of the current Prime Minister, Tony Blair

What's In a Name?

Peter Benjamin Mandelson

One of the main drivers of New Labour

Resigned once, twice, three times a laddish return

Dubbed the *Prince of Darkness* and *Mandy*

But with his shenanigans

Should he be called

Peter Meddlesome instead?

Tales of the Hairdresser

In 2002 there was a media frenzy

Over Cherie Blair, wife of the Prime Minister

Having involved herself with a New Age guru

And the guru's fraudster con-man boyfriend

When purchasing a couple of flats

The Press Secretary, Alastair Campbell

Attempted to do his job as a spin master

But as Alastair and Cherie clashed

Cherie's hairdresser objected to Alistair's tone

To which Alastair replied, *"You mind your own business.*

Remember you're just a fucking hairdresser."

But Wait, There's *Moore*

It was Jo Moore

That on the day

The twin towers fell

Wrote an e-mail stating it was

"....a very good day to get anything

out we want to bury. Councillors' expenses?"

But wait there's more

For there was an allegation

That she later suggested

Releasing damaging figures

On the actual day of

Princess Margaret's funeral

Did this happen?

We might never

Really know the truth

But after *more* than twenty years

Will there be any *more*

Jo Moore?

Betty Boothroyd 1992-2000

Determined and direct

Commanding respect

Through being unbiased

Challenging corruption

In regards to the expenses scandal

She firmly stated, *"Some ministers and MPs*

Have paid more attention to the perks of power

Than their obligations to the nation."

She was the first, and to date, the only

Female Speaker of the House

Her wit, and forthright words

 "... I'm dealing with giants."

Complimenting her dry and distinctive voice

Colourful clothes matching

Her colourful character and personality

Although never a wife

She became a surrogate mother

Scathing and quick-witted in nature

To six hundred and fifty squabbling

Members of parliament

With their childish outbursts

Reprimanding when necessary

Yet always assisting her *children*

To develop and mature

Into humorous and accepting adults

Even in her 90s when she stands up and talks

Other politicians and members of the general public

Listen in awe to her words laced with sincerity

With a genuine measured assessment

She embodies achievement and ambition

Without a ruthless nature that devours so many others

Maintaining dignity and humour in a balanced manner

Ethical and sceptical resulting in wise judgments

Almost fifty years a dedicated politician

But ultimately, always a worker and a woman

Keep it in the Family – Part 2

The *Expenses Scandal* of 2009

Exposed a new level of nepotism

Including using taxpayer's money

To pay their own relatives a salary

The Home Secretary of the Day

Jacqui Smith was one of those

Who was named and shamed

For controversial expenses, which included

Paying her husband £40,000 per year

To be her parliamentary aide

In return he used her password to pay

For two pay-per-view pornographic films

The couple also claimed for

An 88 pence bath tub plug

Which when revealed in the height

Of the *Expenses Scandal,* Jacqui described as

A "… great big personal fuck up"

Jacqui also claimed more than £100,000

Stating that her sister's home was Jacqui's

Main residence, but another scandal

Also haunted Jacqui Smith in 2009

For it was revealed that her husband

Had been writing letters to the newspaper,

Redditch Advertiser praising Jacqui Smith

Without declaring he was her husband

Jacqui certainly taught us

That she is a firm believer

In *Keeping it in the family*

Surviving Scandals

Former MP Keith Vaz

Achieved much in his political career

He was the longest serving British Asian MP

But his longevity perhaps was his ability

To survive scandal after scandal

There were many controversies

Such as his involvement in the Hinduja brothers'

Application for British citizenship

His stance on Salman Rushdie and the *Satanic Verses* book

The allegation of accepting and not declaring

Several thousand pounds from a solicitor

Hinduja Mark II scandal

Having to pay back parliamentary expenses

After revelations during the *Expenses Scandal*

And so many more scandals

Yet the final scandal

Of having unprotected sex

With male prostitutes

And offering to buy them cocaine

Led to his most recent resignation

The political career of Keith Vaz

Was summed up in the *Daily Telegraph*;

"He resigned as a minister in 2001,

Was suspended in 2002

Named in the 2009 expenses scandal!

"Why is Keith Vaz even in parliament?"

Meeting the Public

Just before an election

Politicians do their campaign trails

Speaking to the public and touting for votes

But meeting people does not always go to plan

In 2010 Gordon Brown met Mrs Duffy

Who said, *"And you can't say anything*

About the immigrants ...

All these Eastern Europeans coming in"

Gordon was later driven away but his microphone

Was still on and a private conversation

Regarding Gillian Duffy was heard country-wide

Gordon stated, *"That was a disaster...*

Should never have put me with that woman.

... It's just ridiculous ...

She's just a sort of bigoted woman ..."

When the conversation was played back

To Mrs Gillian Duffy she stated,

"What did I say to be bigoted?"

Gordon was shocked when the recording

Was played back to him live on a radio programme

Resulting in him returning to Rochdale

Visiting Gillian in her home to offer

A private apology and explanation

Could this have been the tipping point

That cost Gordon Brown

And the Labour Party the election?

Duck House

The MP's expenses scandal

Was shocking and disgraceful

Using taxpayer's money

To purchase a *Duck House*

In the middle of a duck island

This was the ultimate display

Of arrogance and hubris

The MP ducked and dived interviews

Resulting in his resignation

As he ducked off from his post

Piggate

An unsubstantiated allegation

Of the Prime Minister of the day

During his earlier university days

Before becoming a member of parliament

Circulated that he had inserted his own *member*

Into a dead pig's mouth

As part of an initiation ceremony

The scandal became known as Piggate

Denials followed

Satirical remarks trickled out

But the authors of the published allegation

Were never sued

And the owner of the alleged photograph

Never brought in front of a court

The now former Prime Minister then endured pig-based
  remarks

Nigel Farage referred to him as *Piggy in the middle*

Nicola Sturgeon referred to him as *Pig-headed*

A distasteful story in the *History of British Politics*

Even though his face could easily have been the flickering

Image between the pigs' and human faces

In a film adaptation of *Animal Farm*

More Than One Way to Skin a Cat

He almost made it to *Father of the House* title

With 49 years as Member of Parliament for Bolsover

Although he maintained he would never

Ever accept such an accolade

However, Dennis became famous

For his straight-talking words

Often getting himself expelled

From the Houses of Parliament

After refusing to withdraw

The adjectives he gave to people's names

Or the insulting nicknames

So perhaps it's time to list

Just some of his quotes

1984: He referred to David Owen as a *Pompous Sod*

1988: *Ey up, here comes Puss in Boots*

To Black Rod, Sir John Gingell

1992: The Minister of Agriculture, John Gummer as

A little squirt of a minister, and

A slimy wart on Margaret Thatcher's nose

And to the Queen he suggested, *Tell her to pay her tax*

2001: *You're nowt but a midget* to Sir Michael Willcocks

2005: *The only thing that was growing then*

Were the lines of coke in front of Boy George....

In reference to the Shadow Chancellor George Osborne

And to the Queen, *Has she brought Camilla with her?*

2006: To the Queen, *Have you brought Helen Mirren on*

standby?

2016: *Dodgy Dave* in reference to Prime Minister, David

Cameron

2017: To the Queen, *Yeah, get your skates on*

First race is at half past two

Although Dennis can give out humour

He is also one of those rare people

Who can also receive humour back

When it was Michael Willcocks'

Last day as Black Rod in 2008

He answered back to Dennis Skinner

I shall miss you, Dennis

But through his entire political career

Dennis Skinner through his pro-Libertarian voting

Pro-Labour stance on working people's rights

Anti-war voting, direct, blunt and candid talking

The *Beast of Bolsover* did indeed prove

That *there's more than one way to skin a cat*

Punch and Judy

The puppet show of *Punch and Judy* has circulated
For over three hundred and fifty years
A glove puppet Mr Punch who beats his wife
His baby, the police and others with a stick

Fast forward to 2001 and a new show was televised
A one-off appearance of *Punches of John Prescott*
As the Deputy Prime Minister punched a man
Who threw an egg at him, reminiscent of *Punch and Judy*

But it was *Punches of Eric Joyce* that was an ongoing saga
In 2012 Eric punched and head-butted his way
Through up to six Conservative Members of Parliament
Then smashed a window as he attempted to resist arrest

Over the next two years the show continued its tour
Across different venues assaulting Airline staff, a teenager
And clashed violently with police again and again
A real life case of, *That's the way to do it?*

Johnson's Journalistic Integrity

He claims that he is not racist

Or homophobic and yet

His journalistic quotes

Includes words and sentences such as

Crowds of flag-waving picanninnies

Tribal warriors will break out in watermelon smiles

Women in burkas who look like letterboxes

Aid-ridden choristers and tank-top bum boys

Boris claims that his quotes

Are wholly satirical

Well following on

From that perspective

Here is satire on his surname

In urban language it means penis

And a penis means that he is a dick

Or an absolute cock

Berlusconism

He encapsulated and modernised all seven deadly sins;

Lust, Gluttony, Greed, Sloth, Wrath, Envy and Pride

His charismatic lifestyle and lustful affairs are well

   publicised

Accusations of orgies, prostitutes, under-aged sex and so

   much more

His lustful affairs were certainly full of gluttony and greed

With old terms such as *Bunga Bunga,* being given a new

   meaning

An appetite that seemed to get greater and greater

For women, girls, wealth, media control, and political

   power

The accusation by Silvio's former wife

Of never attending his own son's eighteenth birthday

Could be an example of sloth, but no doubt time spent

Satisfying his other deadly sins

His wrath showcased when applying pressure to the police

Such as during the *Rubygate* investigation

His rise to power could be based on the sin, envy

A son of middle-class parents

Immersed into a world of corruption, wealth and power

Yet his charismatic allure has given birth to the term,

Berlusconism

The antics, personality, and accusations levelled against
  Silvio
Seem to be extending to other countries and other
  politicians
Perhaps Donald Trump and Boris Johnson should take time
  out
To understand the rise and fall of Silvio Berlusconi
As it could be argued that they are following a similar path
Of the brash and bold Mr Berlusconi

12 Labours of Putin

It was in 2014

That art was created in Russia

Recreating the *Twelve Labours of Hercules*

Only in this version

It was the *Twelve Labours of Vladimir Putin*

Each of the original twelve labours

Reimaged with a young strong Vladimir Putin

Battling the Neamean Lion, the multi-headed Lernaean

    Hydra

The Erymanthian Boar, the Cretan Bull, Cerberus and so on

However, these pieces of art had a twist

Depicting Vladimir Putin's own trials throughout his

    political life

The multi-headed Hydra representing the Europe Union,

The US, Canada and Japan who had imposed sanctions

    against Russia

A macho Herculean Vladimir Putin battling terrorism

Yet the origins of why Hercules performed the twelve

    labours

Was because he had been driven mad

Murdering his own wife and children

The twelve labours were his penance

To reach salvation and retribution

And Hercules was not immortal

He was a demi-God

Born out of an affair

He lived an extraordinary life

But died as dramatically as he lived

So you have to question yourself

Is this the life you really want to emulate?

Modernising Canada

Son of a former Canadian Prime Minister

A privileged youngster

Who carved his own image

Like the tattoos on his body

Of the globe surrounded by a Haida raven

Modern in his attitude and actions

Not just because of his tattoo

Or his admission to taking drugs

But also because

Of his varied and exciting previous jobs

Like a nightclub bouncer

A snowboarding instructor

A high school teacher

And even a charity boxer

Justin Trudeau absorbed the lessons

From his cocktail of professions

And fashioned a new style of politics

Including legalising marijuana

Reducing carbon emissions

An advocate for women's rights

And abortion rights

Introducing legislation for marine conservation

And many, many more innovative policies

Time will tell

Whether any of his three children

Will follow in their father and grandfather's trade

Creating a three-generation dynasty

Of political giants

Angela Merkel

Known as the most powerful woman in the world

Long serving Chancellor of Germany

Whose politics has modernised Europe

And the wider world

Accepting of migrants and freedom

Phasing out nuclear power

Reducing greenhouse gas emissions

Increasing renewable energy

Financially astute as her policies

Directly stimulated worldwide growth

Dealing with crisis after crisis

Including a pandemic

With clarity and professionalism

Her name is Angela Dorothea Merkel

And her place in history is already written

As she is a rare example of a living legend

A chemistry graduate who lit up and enlightened

Germany, Europe and the entire world

Great Britain

From the depths of despair, anger and desolation

Day by day, brick by brick; We lay down the foundation

In order to rise again, and become a great nation

Through times that are rough and tough

We will strive to proceed and succeed

New opportunities we will seek

We will not remain meek or weak

Our strengths we will use

Weaknesses we will reduce

And threats we will defuse

As the links with the EU Union we unweave

History shows us what we can achieve

World wars we have fought and won

The Empire and Commonwealth we have run

Pioneers in ensuring people have their rights

Are just a few of our historical highlights

A new period of negotiation and trade we now face

That future we will boldly and proudly embrace

For we are Great Britain, and that you cannot erase or

   efface

We will gain our premier place through decorum and grace

Courage will ensure we build a new golden age

With the entire globe we are now able to engage

Continue being an essential part of the world stage

Remain or Leave voters and campaigners will unite

With increased passion and vigour we'll show might

Burning fires within our hearts and minds will ignite

As we will reach and create new power and wealth

Invest in our people to promote stability and good health

Despite the prediction of doom and gloom through fear

We will become triumphant because we persevere

Great to Grate

It's time to reflect upon what has happened and the truth to
finally orate

For weeks campaigners argued 'remain' or 'leave' and
gave it to us straight

All those many days where men and women engaged in
heated debate

In order to decide the future of Great Britain in the
European Union state

Boris, Farage, and Cameron all say they want to make
Britain Great

To the polls the people go, to cast their vote and a
referendum decision to create

Through the night voters listen to their television screens
making bedtime very late

Graphs of the voting, like in a General Election, they
continue to show in order to illustrate

Then the outcome is announced and those in favour of EU
'Leave' now start to celebrate

Unaware of what is about to transpire to Great Britain,
Great Britain, Great...

The pound, hour by hour, begins its decline and its strength
does depreciate
The value of stocks and shares not only fluctuate but
actually just decimate
Experts discuss on the news what will occur to the bank's
interest rate
An isolated island. All alone. Abandoned. Desolate.
Once known as Britain. A nation that was great.

But weep for all those who left loved ones and to Britain
did migrate
Wanting a better life, but now become victims of
campaigns of hate
Ignorant people, hiding behind cowardly written notes,
demanding others to repatriate
Did you think there would be no consequence for the
voting bomb that you did detonate?
A once tolerant nation. No longer considered to be great.

The decline continues with speed and does accelerate
The EU demanding Article 50 and to immediately
disassociate
So that they become twenty-seven countries instead of
twenty-eight

Foreign companies their headquarters to other countries
they will relocate
In one fell swoop Britain is shredded. Great Britain. Grate
Britain. Grate….

Motherhood

You tweeted about your *motherhood* comments

With total conviction you tried to alter the contents

"Truly appalling and the exact opposite of what I said.

I am disgusted." Perhaps the transcript you should have
read

Then you held a press conference and this is what you
orated

To try to stop yourself from becoming a candidate that is
hated

"I was repeatedly asked about my children and I repeatedly
made it clear"

You are now trying to make it appear as though your words
they smear

"That I did not want this in any way to be a feature of the
campaign"

But the initial *motherhood* words you did speak has caused
so much pain

Question: "What is the main difference between you and
Theresa May?"

Answer: "… A huge member of a huge family …" You

really do dismay

"I was repeatedly asked about my children." NO. NO. NO.
The evidence is there. You are now causing so much woe
"I don't want this to be Andrea has children, Theresa
    doesn't"
Then why say that? Uttering words of poison you shouldn't

"Genuinely, I feel that being a mum means you have a real
    stake
In the future of our country." Your words really make me
    quake
"I want to be crystal clear that everyone has an equal stake
in our society and in the future of our country." That's the
    remake

"But I have children who are going to have children." Now
    a prophet!
Your children you should be proud of. Not use them for
    political profit
"But I have children." Which means you had sex and then
    became pregnant
Then you gave birth like a cat or a dog, an ant or an
    elephant

"But I have **children.** I have **children.** I have children. I
have children"
So say those words to someone going through IVF who is
barren
There is no excuse Mrs Andrea Leadsom
Those words you uttered are pure loathsome

Sparring Partners

There are many famous sparring partners

For those old enough to remember

Big Daddy versus Giant Haystacks

J.R. Ewing versus Cliff Barnes

Alexis Colby versus Krystal Carrington

Edward Heath versus Margaret Thatcher

Margaret Thatcher versus Neil Kinnock

Margret Thatcher versus Arthur Scargill

They have wonderful criticising words

Which they deliver with precision

Often cutting and scathing remarks

Riling up their adversary

Perhaps the sparring rivalry

Between Nicola Sturgeon and Ruth Davidson

Sums up the volcanic relationships

When Ruth delivers the words,

"I won't take any lessons from the First Minister"

At which point Nicola rises to respond and is met with

Ruth Davidson's dismissing hand and the words

"Because actually, sit down …

… I will not take another intervention"

Her vocabulary being reminiscent and authoritative

As the dog handler and breeder, Barbara Woodhouse

Uttering to dogs her famous words, "Sii-IITT"

Ultimate Father of the House

There have been many

Who have occupied the title

Father of the House

The revered and respected

Longest serving Member of Parliament

But one stands out

As the embodiment of that position

Instantly recognisable

After 49 years as an MP

With his jovial and humorous exchanges

Passionately championing his beliefs

Debating with mutual respect

Able to encompass the old-fashioned concept of humility

Knowing how to compromise

Boasting and exploding with common sense

Common sense in his pragmatic words

Which are easily understood by all

Always behaving with integrity

He is a political giant

Known as *The Big Beast of British Politics*

Whose blood might be Conservative blue

But has earned the respect of the general public

Regardless of which party or policies they support

He is listened to without the usual pantomime reactions

With qualities that are exceptionally rare for a politician to
possess;

Trustworthy, authentic, plausible, reliable and genuine

In fact you would struggle to find another politician

Who possesses those qualities and standards

And his name

His name is Kenneth Clarke

Dancing Queen

She showed us her dance moves

In Africa and at a Conservative Party conference

Brave and audacious considering she cannot dance

Not even to a 'mum dancing' standard

Instead hers arms jolt up and down

As though a prototype robot

Attempting to learn dancing

You can almost hear clog wheels churning

Which need lubricating with oil or WD40

Limbs moving without any rhythm

Almost like being electrocuted

Spasm after spasm

Through routines that look

Like exercises for OAPs

Rather than dancing

Awkward smiles

Trying to mask her dread

Because her legs might as well

Be made from iron or lead

Dancing Queen

(Extended Version)

She showed us her dance moves

In Africa and at a Conservative Party conference

Brave and audacious considering she cannot dance

Not even to a 'mum dancing' standard

Instead she is a cross between a prototype robot

With slow-moving robotic arms

Attached onto a female version of Mr Soft

From the spearmint soft mints adverts

Virtually creating a bride for Frankenstein's Monster

Although this *Dancing Queen* is already married

To a devoted husband, Sir Philip May

And we may assume he is no Frankenstein

Not eight foot tall nor a bolt through his neck

You can almost hear clog wheels churning

Which need lubricating with oil

Or WD40 added to her elbows

Her limbs move without any rhythm

Almost like being electrocuted

Spasm after spasm

Through routines that look

Like exercises for OAPs

Rather than dancing

Awkward smiles

Trying to mask her dread

Because her legs might as well

Be made from iron or lead

Brexit

Brave words of Brexit

Spoken over and over

"We are leaving on the 29th of March 2019"

"We will be leaving on October 31st, Deal or No Deal"

"Brexit means Brexit"

"We need to get on and deliver Brexit"

"No deal is better than a bad deal"

"No deal is catastrophic for this country"

"We hold all the cards"

"It is not in the interests of the European Union"

"The free trade agreement … with the European Union …

… will be one of the easiest in human history"

"It is the will of the people"

"I represent my constituents"

"There will be no changes to the backstop"

"The backstop needs to go"

"This house needs to…"

"I will not ask for an extension"

"I will abide by the law"

"I strongly disagree with the judgment of the judiciary"

"If you have not secured a deal will you request an

    extension?"

"I am not inclined to do so"

"It needs to go to a people's vote"

"The people have spoken"

"I represent the people"

"This is a dead parliament"

"This is a paralysed parliament"

"The Prime Minister needs to resign"

"The Opposition Leader needs to resign"

"I have removed the Tory Whip"

"We are united as one"

"This is a domestic issue for the United Kingdom"

"I will be pushing for a second referendum on Scottish
Independence"

"It is unconstitutional to prorogue parliament"

"We need to prorogue parliament because we need a
Queen's speech"

"Will the Prime Minister apologise to Her Majesty for
misleading her?"

"There is only one chlorinated chicken in this house"

It is the rollercoaster ride of political satire

That has become known across the world as Brexit

Hunt

His name is Jeremy Hunt

On the premiership he took a punt

But came second place in that stunt

His name is Jeremy Hunt

When he sat on the benches at the front

The NHS he tried to decimate and confront

His name is Jeremy Hunt

Let me make this clear and blunt

Some say his name aptly rhymes with ….

Boris

Boris, Borys or Barys

All originate from Bulgar

The Bulgars was a tribe

Known as the Old Great Bulgaria

Bulgar is also a language;

Oghur Turkic which is where

We find the meaning of the name

Bori in Turkic meant wolf

Borgori meant short

Bars was a snow leopard

Borislav meant battle

It is a name that is particularly prevalent

In Bulgaria, Hungary, Russia, Siberia and Alaska

If you are named Boris it looks like

You have a secret savageness to your nature

Creating enemies, and battle after battle

Where you unleash the wolf and the snow leopard in you

Because victory, wealth and empire-building

Is all that you understand

Campaign Elections

No, no. I never said that.

Well, yes okay.

But that's out of context.

Can't we talk about my policies?

Let's get Brexit done.

No the NHS is not for sale.

Never said that.

No. Oh.

My campaign leaflets haven't been delivered.

Here's the proof.

No I can't supply the addresses.

I want my deposit back.

I want a free second drop of my literature.

I'm suing the Royal Mail and my opponents.

I'm for the people.

Vote for me. VOTE FOR ME. VOTE …

Rise of the Phoenix

Name: Boris Johnson

Career Credentials:

Dismissed from *The Times* for Lying

Dismissed from Government for lying

Fame: Unfaithful to his wives AND lying

Number of Children: at least … erm ... dunno

Main Motto: erm, delay, no dither, erm, ah yes

Name: Dominic Cummings

Career Credentials:

Dismissed by Prime Minister Theresa May

Fame: Special Advisor AND Slogans

Driving to Barnard Castle during lockdown

Number of Children: Have sympathy for me, I have a four-year-old

Main Motto: I acted legally and reasonably

Frosty Reception

A journalist

Trying his best

To obtain an interview

With the Prime Minister

Just before a General Election

A minder of the Prime Minister

Mouths a swear word that is pre-watershed

Followed by the Prime Minster stating

"I'll be with you in a second.

I'll be with you in a second."

Before he walks away

Into a milk fridge

Where he hides

Rather than face an interview

Perhaps your image

Would have been less frosty

Had you merely been truthful

That you had no intention

Of being interviewed

Than lying yet again

Twice in a few seconds

Accusations About and Against Arcuri

Yet another juicy story

Regarding Boris and his conquests

Did they or didn't they have an affair?

Did he or did he not influence the grants

That were given to Jennifer Arcuri?

The media speculated and gave out

Dates and times when Boris and Jennifer

Were together and the amounts given to Arcuri

The late night visits to Jennifer's apartment

The free speeches and accompanying Johnson

On trade missions that had previously been declined

Eventually, Jennifer goes live on *Good Morning Britain*

Where Piers Morgan asked a direct question

"Did you ever have any intimate relationship

With Boris Johnson? Yes or no?"

To which Jennifer gave her answer

"And because the press have made me this objectified

Ex-model pole dancer, I'm really not going to answer

That question." But what happened later

Made even more entertaining television

Lorraine Kelly before explaining what would happen

On her own show said, *"Yeah. God that was crazy*

Wasn't it. That was ... what was the point? Come down

And not answer any questions." Piers offered the opportunity

For Jennifer to respond but was annihilated by Lorraine

Who persisted, *"You didn't answer any of the questions*

That were put to you and I just don't see the point.

I don't see the point of you coming on. Anyway, ..."

And with those words Lorraine cut Jennifer no more

Air time as she continued to explain the contents of her own

show

Migrating Birds

Immigration rules to be updated

Following Brexit from the EU.

What have migrating birds got to offer?

We have enough birds contributing to the environment.

Do they have unique skills?

Will they be able to contribute to the economy?

Or will they just be eating our food supplies?

Will they be using the twigs from United Kingdom trees?

Building their own homes and shelter without permission

Almost as though squatters.

Scavenging the soil to locate British worms.

We are a sovereign nation now.

Birds wanting to migrate to Britain

Will need to meet new regulatory rules.

All birds caught that are illegal immigrants

Will be investigated, tagged and sent back to where they

came from.

Those who migrate legally are welcome

So long as they immerse themselves in our culture.

And under no circumstances are they allowed to chirp in

their ethnic language.

Chirp the Queen's English.

In fact, learn to chirp the British National Anthem.

Rainbow

They say that history does repeat itself

Boris Johnson trying to be Prime Ministerial

By imitating his hero, Winston Churchill

But has instead become Bungle Boris

A boastful, blagging and blithering bear

Suggesting we should be in awe of his *"success"*

Matt Hancock wearing his pale pink tie

At the Daily Briefings where he has become

Jittery and tentative as George the pink hippo

Still giving out advice, such as watching her *"tone"*

Priti Patel, when not elusive, is as lippy as Zippy

Defining her image with her *"Herculean efforts"*

But there is no calm and sensible Geoffrey

Instead the quartet has a fourth puppet

Or perhaps that should that be muppet?

As Dominic Rabb stands tall and proud

With the strength of a mountain gorilla

Explaining his glory at being a Tory

The innocence from the 1970s and 1980s

Has been lost in this new version of Rainbow

Allegedly written by Dominic Cummings

A horrific and terrifying modern retelling

As they recreate an unbelievable narrative

Presenting themselves as heroic saviours

Priti to Pretty

Her name is Priti Patel

Arguably, one hell of a girl

Wanting to bring back

The death penalty

Deporting people

As many as she can

Gloating that even her own parents

Would have been deported

If coming to the UK now

Her swagger is confident

Standing on a black box

To elevate her height

In front of the podium

To echo her perceived status

As the Queen of the Cabinet

Aspiring to go even higher

Explaining her "Herculean efforts"

But all her claims to valour

Are as mythical as her analogy

Yes, her name is Priti Patel

But what's pretty about her?

Accused of bullying

Of humiliating workers

The monstrous defence;

That her actions were "unintentional"

That she was unaware of the effects

Yet she also has fame

For smirking and laughing

Almost like the pigs from *Animal Farm*

And hence a queen of No Respect

Her name is Priti Patel

But there's nothing special

Or pretty there

The Final Nail

The first nail:

Decimating the share price

The second one:

Ignoring previous legally signed agreements

Third Nail:

Ignoring the unions

Fourth Nail

Brutal restructuring

Nail after nail

Each one representing

Every disastrous decision

Creating a blame culture

Bringing in cutthroat personnel

Driving up conduct code cases

Increasing dismissals

Numbers of employment tribunal cases spiralling

Not paying a dividend

Whilst claiming all of his own salary

And additional benefits

Not reporting to financial markets or shareholders

Becoming a dictator instead of a leader

Incapable of inspiring others

Until the final nail is hammered

Deep into the coffin

The nail representing

Staff being sent to work

Without the correct PPE

As he stays at home

Self-isolating in luxury

Benefiting whilst others work

Pillar box red blood spilled

As workers work and work

Exhausted to the extreme

In the most dangerous conditions

Since the Second World War

Let the Share Price Go Up

Share price started to decimate when you arrived

Your staff of a decent wage you cruelly deprived

You received a £6 million handshake hello

Because money and greed is all that you know

You refused to acknowledge previous agreements

Resulting in union disputes and disagreements

You sacked established director after director

Then blatantly became a major investor

Announcements you made to decimate the share price

Which was all part of your cunning and devious device

To buy and buy shares at a reduced and rock bottom price

And so the shareholders and staff you actually did sacrifice

And when there was a crisis like no other seen before

You seized the opportunity to game play some more

Your staff you sent out during the Coronavirus War

Whilst pocketing millions for your account offshore

You destroyed a flagship company

But your resignation today luckily

Means that the company can thrive again

Which we will endeavour to sustain

Let the staff start to feel relieved

No more bullying and feeling aggrieved

Let hardworking staff be rewarded

And the former CEO be deported

Let the bad times be eradicated

No longer feeling tired and deflated

Let the share price and morale increase

A place of work to be happy and in peace

Three Part Slogans

Stay at Home

Protect the NHS

Save Lives

Stay Alert

Control the Virus

Save Lives

Herd Immunity: All Animals are Equal

Some are more equal than others

"If that means some pensioners die, too bad"

Dear Dominic

You are out of touch with reality

Out of touch with the people of Great Britain

Unelected, ungracious, and utterly ignorant

Your damage control interview

Has damaged you more than you realise

This is just the beginning

Of people getting even angrier

At your lack of remorse

Lack of understanding other people's sacrifices

And lack of adherence to the spirit of the rules

You are trying to demonise the press

For bringing this to light

Trying to get sympathy from the public

For all those hard decisions

That you have to do, day in and day out

For which you are paid so well to deliver on

Despite the lack of PPE

You are striving for sympathy

Poor, poor Dominic

Living in a house on private land

And private woodland

Where the nearest neighbour is half a mile away

Saying you drove to the Castle

To see if you were able to drive 270 miles

Because you had been so unwell

Surely, driving that amount of miles

When you are not sure if you are capable of driving

Suggests you don't care about other drivers either

Just wait until Prime Minister's Question Time

That's going to be explosive once the MPs are back

p.s. Dear Dominic,

Do you not realise

That demonising the press

For all these years

Means that you are also demonising

The Commissioning Editor of *The Spectator*

Who just happens to be your wife

Writing the Narrative

When you are used to writing the narrative

Expert in spin, in hiding and lurking

A genuine Svengali who smirks

Proud of his achievements

Brutal against others

Believing that he comes across as sincere

That people will believe whatever nonsense he says

A complete control freak

Sociopathic and cruel

Yet totally oblivious to the reality

That people have their own opinions

No matter how much he wants to write the narrative

With emotive slogans to tug at emotions

That ultimately each one of us

Is capable of writing our very own narrative

We live our own lives and make our own decisions

The DC Solution

I'm not talking about DC Comics

Where Batman fights the Joker

And Superman beats Lex Luther

I'm on about Dominic Cummings

And the whole DC Debacle

The Prime Minister of New Zealand

Jacinta Ardern took a 20% pay cut

During the Global Coronavirus Pandemic

As did all her ministers

Whereas in the UK the ministers

Had an increase of £10,000

To the costs they were allowed to claim

In order to set up working from home

Dominic Cummings did not act reasonably

Despite both Boris and Dominic claiming he did

A large percentage of the public and MPs

Want either Dominic to resign

Or Boris to sack his mate

However, there is a medium solution

If Boris wants to save his Special Advisor

Then perhaps like footballers

There should be a penalty

Not a yellow card as such

But for Dominic to take one month out

Without pay to reflect and review his actions

Furloughed staff lost at least 20% of their pay

It is a small sacrifice for Dominic

To take time out

And in the long term return to his job

Fuck You

There is an unwritten rule

Known as *Fuck You*

Johnson will fuck woman after woman

Get them pregnant and move on

Deny his relationship with them

And move on

Whereas Cummings

No pun with the cum

Actually creates contentious slogans

£350 million for the NHS

Stay at Home, Protect the NHS, Save Lives

Flouts and breaks his own slogans

And so *Fucks Over*

The entire British nation

Dead Cats and Live Horses

They use the dead cat strategy

To divert the public's attention

But one dead cat is not enough

And so another is thrown in out

And another, and another

But it's way too late

For the horse has bolted

Literally galloped

From London

All the way to Durham

And then gently trotted

For an excursion

To Barnard Castle

Coincidences

On the 12th of April 2020

Dominic Cummings drove his wife

And son to Barnard Castle to test his eyesight.

That date just happens to be his wife's birthday.

A fact which he neglected to mention

In his one-hour-plus press interview.

Happy belated 45th birthday Mary Wakefield

(wife of Dominic Cummings).

Was it really worth celebrating your 45th birthday

270 miles away from your primary residence?

And then going out for a trip to Barnard Castle?

Another coincidence which skipped Dominic's mind

At the one-hour-plus press conference

Was that at Barnard Castle there is a factory

Of GlaxoSmithKline which TWO DAYS after Dominic's
  visit

Announced their contract to develop a Covid-19 vaccine

This is a company which in the past was fined $3 billion

For fraud, overcharging and making false claims

Not to mention a £37.6 million fine for bribing other
  companies

Perhaps the above two 'coincidences'

Should have been explored further?

Instead Dominic has become

The subject of comedians' dreams

As the comedic jokes have spread

Far wider than Dominic's original

270 mile trip during the first lockdown

By YOUR Logic

Quotes from YOUR own website suggests

"Courses such as Politics, Philosophy and Economics

(and Economics in general) do not train political leaders

   well.

They encourage superficial bluffing, misplaced

   confidence".

You go on to say

"Many default to gimmicks and attempts to manipulate the

   media."

(Dominic Cummings Blog, My essay on an 'Odyssean'

Education, 2013/2014).

These above quotes

From YOUR own blog

Summarise ALL of your contribution to political life

I do NOT wish the Cummings family any ill feeling

Or hatred in a world which can be cruel

A world that can be vindictive and judgemental

However, you should accept responsibility for your actions

What you did was NOT in the national interest

It was NOT as stated in your press conference

It was NOT within the spirit of the rules

You should APOLOGISE for your error of judgement

A little humility

A reality check

With a simple heartfelt apology

When so many HAVE adhered to the rules

When so many HAVE suffered

When they have encountered hardships

Would have gone a long, long way

My fear is that you've left it too late

Any apology now

Will be viewed as just one more lie

Trickling from your mouth

Cronyism and Coronavirus Contracts

The Coronavirus pandemic
Highlighted the extent of cronyism
When giving out taxpayer's money
To specified companies and people
Who had personal ties and former links
To Government ministers, the Prime Minister
And the *Special Advisor* Dominic Cummings

The Government cut bureaucracy
No ethical tendering processes
Lack of transparency
Normal declarations of assets and links
Hidden and undeclared
Individuals and companies benefitting
From friendships and previous donations

Slowly, slowly
The media uncovers and reveals
Alleged blatant corruption
But as yet
No repercussions
Other than millions of pounds in profits
And thousands more excess deaths

Bullying Buddies of Boris

It has been recorded in newspapers

That there had been ongoing bullying

By Boris' mate, Dominic Cummings

And Dominic's allies against Boris' fiancée

Allegations that they referred to Carrie Symonds

As *Princess Nut,* and even put emojis

Of a princess and then two nuts and two nuts again

When referring to Carrie by text

One article also stated that Carrie was referred to

As Cersei from *Game of Thrones*

The newspaper articles claim that this went on for months

To be fair to Boris, Dominic and Carrie

Their shenanigans and ongoing saga

Does seem to be like *Game of Thrones*

But does that mean Boris is the Iron King, Robert
  Baratheon

A bulky arrogant King whose tally of conquests of women

And bastard children he has sired are both unknown

Dominic Cummings could then be Theon Greyjoy

From a rich and powerful dynasty

Who becomes arrogant and cocky

Until he is tortured and emancipated

No longer an arrogant cock

Echoing the departure of Dominic from Downing Street

His power and arrogance now severed

Hypocrisy and Irony – Part 1

You give the politicians verbal heat

Your vacant heart replaced

With a mound of your newspaper articles

Slowly rotting away

As it's black printed words seep

Becoming journalistic blood

Running through your veins

The words that you used

Regarding Dominic Cummings

And his trip to Durham and Barnard Castle

"He's single-handedly destroyed the lockdown"

"He's destroyed trust in the government.

He needs to go.

God knows what Cummings had on Boris."

"Every part of this story stinks."

Dominic's trip was 270 miles

But in December 2020 your trip was far, far, longer

When only essential travel was permitted

You went to Antigua

I remind you of the words you used earlier in the year

"By doing what he did, refusing to even apologise
Refusing to admit that anything he did was wrong.
Even though none of us could do what he did."
"Why shouldn't I pull a Cummings?"
His decisions *"will cost lives"*

Your actions, lack of an apology
And your justification remarks
Are just pure hypocrisy
Where is your sacrifice?
What about what you said
About not putting your parents' lives at risk?
Think of the message you have sent
Concerning the spirit of lockdown measures

There is also an irony
That your initials are *P.M.*
Oh what a thought
Piers Morgan for Prime Minister
Vote for me. Vote for me. VOTE …

After such a chilling thought
I'll think I'll have a rum
And there's the second irony
For you are no Captain Morgan either

Hypocrisy and Irony – Part 2

If we look at politicians and their history

Across the world in each and every country

It's not hard to find examples of hypocrisy

Giving rise to comments full of irony

Inflaming the viewers and readers with fury

In a world where we should be kind instead of nasty

Be empathetic and of your political status be worthy

Instead of jeering and showcasing traits that are ugly

You come across as murky, shitty, and unworthy

And that's the same from each and every political party

To become truly revered and trusted is no mystery

Just stop trying to score points on being funny

Be ethical, truthful, transparent, virtuous, and deliver

honestly

In order to avoid being accused of irony and hypocrisy

Politicians and the Press

Politicians and the press
It's a love-hate relationship
They need each other
But are very rarely faithful
Towards one another

The politicians want the press
To give them credibility
And the press want the truth
As they dig away with journalistic techniques
Discovering juicy hidden secrets

Yet there have been occasions
When the press have become the news
Robert Maxwell and Rupert Murdoch
Newspapers sued for compensation
Accusations of fake news

When litigation happens
It's like an uncomfortable and disputed
Divorce or legal separation
Where arguments are made

To try and claim as many assets as possible

Yet once the litigation is over
The relationship soon flares up again
No longer legally married
But friends with benefits
As they continue to try and influence each other

Fishy Things

The last two First Ministers of Scotland

Were Alex Salmond and Nicola Sturgeon

The original meaning of Salmond

Is *Son of Solomon* but there is also a theory

That the word *salmond* is an old and obsolete word

For the fish salmon, and *sturgeon* of course is a fish

Scotland has vast amounts of fish in their waters

Fish are slippery and scaly with strong odours

Their slipperiness can make them hard to catch

When the politicians Salmond and Sturgeon

Become passionate or enraged about what

They are discussing it is almost as though

Their necks expand, showcasing absent gills

And their faces become as pink as the flesh of salmon

There are also ancient Scottish tales of selkies

Creatures that could change from seals to humans

By shedding their seal skin and many adventures followed

There were even several oral tales that the selkies

Had affairs galore resulting in many hybrid children

Half-selkie and half-human with webbed toes or fingers

Just asking, but has anyone actually ever seen the toes of

   Alex or Nicola?

She Disappears Again

Whenever there is a crisis

She disappears

Returns at the point

When she has been criticised

For her non-appearances

And when things seems to be

Turning a corner for the better

She gives herself her own accolades

Including her *Herculean efforts*

Yet where is her apology?

For the accusations of bullying

For the loss of 400,000 criminal records

From the Police National Computer system

Perhaps Priti Patel

It's time to say farewell

Again

Thank You and Goodbye

Virtually fifty years after Enoch Powell's

Controversial and infamous *Rivers of Blood* speech

Where he put forward the opinion

Of paying ethnic minorities £2,000 each

To leave the United Kingdom

As part of a resettlement figure

To return to their country of origin

Are we now one step closer to that ideology

Becoming a reality?

But without a payment

Just a *thank you and goodbye*

The *Windrush generation scandal* being just the start

Will the European Union Settlement Scheme (EUSS)

Eventually, be discovered to have also

Led to vulnerable people who had a right to stay

Being deported from the United Kingdom?

Or will the *get tough on immigration* stance

Of Priti Patel and her vision soften?

The Savage and Sensational She-Sulk

A bulky Ted Heath

When he lost his premiership role

Earned the nickname

The Incredible Sulk

A comparison between himself

And Marvel's *Incredible Hulk*

In recent months

Theresa May for her criticism

Of her heir to the Prime Minister role

Is receiving the same critique

But is she Marvel's *Savage She-Sulk?*

Or a glamorous *Sensational She-Sulk?*

A lost opportunity regarding

The Incredible Sulks

Was Gordon Brown's working relationship

With his Prime Minister, Tony Blair

Ultimately to avoid the flair up of the green-eyed monster

Just, *Don't make them angry*

Doom With Zoom

It's been almost one year
Since Zoom became part
Of many people's lives
In order to communicate

It was in December 2020
When Handforth Parish Council
Held an extraordinary meeting
That the following month went viral

We saw the backs of some Parish counsellors
Tempers descending and raging into anger
Accusations, reprimands and lots of shouting
And not forgetting the ejection of the Chairman

"I was thrown out of the meeting."
"Quite rightly."
 "Will you stop talking."
"Will you stop being whatever it is you're trying to be."
Julie's iPad: *"Yeah. I'm just in a meeting at the moment.*
Can I give you a call back when it finishes?"

"Who is Jackie Weaver?"

"This meeting has not been called according to the law."

"Mrs Weaver please."

"You have no authority Jackie Weaver, no authority at all."

"This is a disgrace."

"She's kicked him out."

"This is a meeting called by two councillors."

"Illegally."

"You may now elect a Chair."

"No they can't because the Vice-Chair's here. I take charge."

"Read the standing orders. READ THEM AND UNDERSTAND THEM."

"Dear me."

"Appalling behaviour."

"You don't know what you are talking about."

"Hahahahaha. Hahahahaha. Hahahahaha."

"We're trying to have a Teams meeting you fool."

"Call me Britney Spears."

Ironically, she hit that button *one more time*

Ejecting the Chairman once again

Although an investigation is underway
You have entertained the entire world
But I do have one more *"point of order"*
Will any of you ever get elected
Just *"one more time?"*

Burps and Farts

When will you learn?

Once you let out

A burp or a fart

That's out there now

And cannot

Be taken back

Rudy is Rude

Rudy Giuliani

In the Borat sequel

Frequently smiling at Tutar

With a leathery bloated aged face

Showing his expensive dentures

Reminiscent of a crocodile or shark

A predator ready for his salacious meal

Patting Tutar on her legs

Old and experienced hands

On tender, juicy meat

Rudy Giuliani

Going into a hotel bedroom

With Borat's *daughter, Tutar*

Asking for her phone number and address

Patting her as she is bent over

Making himself comfortable on the bed

Clothes untucked and fidgeting

An ancient relic ready for action

Siphoning off the elixir of youth

Until her father arrives to save the day

Concede

When Joe Biden took the lead

And President Elect he did succeed

Trump refused to politely concede

Instead to the courts he did proceed

To dispute the results with speed

Because that man is full of greed

He doesn't care if the US does bleed

He then went to his golf club I believe

Where the wind finally proved his hair does recede

It's a wig. It's a wig. We're finally all agreed

Political Firsts

It's usually highly regarded to be

The first to do something in the world of politics

The first British female Prime Minister

The first black President of the United States of America

The first female Chancellor of Germany

The first Muslim Mayor of London

And many, many more examples of political firsts

When becoming a political first

It is often highly regarded because

You have broken barriers to prejudice

Whether it be sex discrimination, race discrimination

Or some other form of discrimination

And yes, this is stating the very *bleedin' obvious*

However, occasionally

You become a political first

For something that is negative

It can be embarrassing

For example, being the first

President of the United States of America

To be impeached twice is not exactly

The accolade or legacy that anyone would want

Hypocrisy and Irony – Part 3

In November 2020

When the report on Priti Patel's

Alleged bullying was published

The report stated that there were

Instances where Priti Patel

Had shouted and sworn at staff

But that she had not *intentionally*

Meant to have caused distress

After the publication of the report

Boris Johnson defended Priti Patel

Insisting that she had NOT broken

The Ministerial Code and that

She had not been made aware

Of the impact of her behaviour

The vehement support of Priti Patel

By Boris Johnson and his insistence

That the matter was now closed

Led to the resignation of Sir Alex Allan

Yet the conclusion of the report

And the reaction of Boris Johnson

Is not that far removed from the infamous

Princess Diana and Martin Bashir *Panorama* interview

In which internal BBC investigations continued

To cover up the full extent of the deceitful nature

In which Martin Bashir managed to obtain

Access to Princess Diana and fuelled

Her internal battle with fear, paranoia, and isolation

Yet when Boris Johnson was interviewed on this matter

He ironically and hypocritically stated that he was

"obviously concerned" about the findings

Can he and the public not see that his reaction

To the Priti Patel report on alleged bullying

Is virtually reminiscent of the BBC's internal findings

On the complaints of how Martin Bashir obtained the
  interview

The only difference is the fine line between

Martin Bashir's deliberate and calculated

Method of fraud and lies

And Priti Patel's blatant shouting and swearing

But that her *intent* was not to cause harm

But merely an indication of her frustration

Chemistry

Chemistry

It's a word

That is not associated

With politics or politicians

And yet it is an element

That exists deep-rooted

In the history and future

Of politics

Margaret Thatcher

And Angela Merkel

The first female British Prime Minster

And the first female Chancellor of Germany

Both having studied chemistry

In their university years

It is the combination

Of chemistry and charisma

A bright and colourful personality

That politicians possess

Which gets them votes

To be elected

Whilst the dull

Often disappear

But it is the chemistry

Of another kind in politics

That often makes the biggest headlines

The chemistry of their love lives

Salacious and secret extra-marital affairs

That are exposed by the media

In an explosive and dramatic manner

Echoing a chemistry experiment

Analysed and written about

To a dissertation level

Husbands and Wives

of Prime Ministers

Husbands and wives

Of British Prime Minsters

Are in the background

Supporting their spouse

Often depicted in newspapers

And of course *Spitting Image*

Mary Wilson was wife of Prime Minister,

Harold Wilson for fifty-five years until his death in 1995

Mary was strong as she held her own views

Opposing her husband in the referendum

For continued membership and integration in Europe

Supported the Campaign for Nuclear Disarmament

She was a poet and had two volumes published

At the age of 97 she accepted an invitation

To Margaret Thatcher's funeral

She became the first, and to date the only

Prime Minister's spouse to reach the age

Of one hundred years old

Audrey Callaghan held her own careers

But in July 2001 her Alzheimer's condition

Worsened and she entered a nursing home

Her husband, James Callaghan, visited her daily

Until her death in March 2005

Eleven days later James also passed away

They were a true example

Of a devoted and dedicated husband and wife

Together on earth for over seventy years

There was Dennis Thatcher

Often shown as swilling

And spilling his wine in *Spitting Image*

He summed up his marriage with the words,

"For forty years I have been married

To one of the greatest women

The world has ever produced.

All I could produce – small as it may be –

Was love and loyalty."

In an interview Dennis explained that being

The husband to the Prime Minister meant

"The longer you keep your mouth shut,

The safer you are."

Norma Major was quiet

Got on with dressmaking

Charity work and wrote two books

The media revelation of her husband's former affair

Was dealt with in her normal quiet and devoted manner

The Majors' marriage survived due to their commitment

Whilst Edwina's character was scrutinised

Making new money out of an affair

That happened over a decade earlier

Surely a movie just waiting to be made

Next up was Cherie Blair

Far louder, brash and opinionated

Than her predecessor

Speaking with verve on any matter

Including her opinion

On those who worked with her husband

One could almost say that her abilities

Concerning speeches and interviews

Clearly show that she is the daughter of an actor

Are the Times A-Changin'?

Come gather round and ask yourself

Are the times really a-changin'?

Or does history keep repeating itself

No lessons learned from the past

Instead doomed to repeat and repeat

The clashes of miners and police

In the era of Thatcher and Scargill

Repeated in the *yellow vest* clashes in France

And other demonstrations across the world

Including invading Congress in January 2021

Come gather round and ask yourself

Are the times really a-changin'?

Women being equal to men

Treated with respect by the men they work with

Margaret Thatcher ousted as Prime Minster

By the men in her own party

Tears flowin' as she leaves Downing Street

Years later, the second female Prime Minster of the UK

Also criticised by the male MPs in her own party

Eventually resigning and more tears as she leaves Number
  Ten

Come gather round and ask yourself

Are the times really a-changin'?

In Ancient Rome

Brothels, extra-marital affairs, and orgies

Were prevalent and rife in ordinary life

Amongst politicians, the elite and their wives

Fast forward over two thousand years

The rumours and anecdotes of Silvio Berlusconi

His affairs, orgies and bunga bunga rituals

Seem to show that little has changed

So, cum gather round and ask yourself

Are the times really a-changin'?

Tears of a Clown

Tears of a clown

By Smokey Robinson and the Miracles

Seems more pertinent now

To lives of the politicians

Now if there's a smile on my face

It's only there to fool the public

.... Don't let my sad expression

Give you the wrong impression

.... Like a clown I appear to be glad

.... The tears of a clown

When there's no one around

Only in today's society

Politicians are not averse

To shedding a tear

When the cameras are rolling

And there's certainly

Plenty of people around

To see those sad, sad, tears

Barack Obama

Vladimir Putin

Kim Jong Un

Justin Trudeau

George W Bush

Silvio Berlusconi

Aung San Suu Kyi

Cristina Fernandez de Kirchner

Margaret Thatcher

Theresa May

Matt Hancock

Genuine tears

Or sinister tears

Aimed at gaining

Your sympathy

And your future votes

Are those tears *sad, sad, sad*

Or merely *bad, bad, bad*

... Only there

Trying to fool the public?

Legacy

Your actions and reactions

Words you have spoken

How you conduct yourself

Keeping calm or showing anger

Restraining your emotions

Dealing with major events

Including crisis and catastrophes

Serving the public instead of yourself

Are just a few of the elements

That will define your place in history

For every single person is mortal

But being a politician

Means you will leave a legacy

A legacy that will be admired

Or a legacy that will be shamed and ridiculed

Eternal Legacy

There are very few in life

Whose name eventually

Becomes an actual word

For which they are famous for

And becomes a word

That is used in everyday language

Casanova was an actual man

Whose name has become synonymous

With being a womaniser

A lover who is promiscuous

Adonis was a character from Greek myth

He had various stories attributed to him

But it was his handsome and physical attributes

That gave rise to the word now meaning

A handsome man whose physique is perfect

Mata Hari

Was an exotic dancer

A prostitute

Convicted of being a spy

Executed by a firing squad

At the age of 41

If you are described as a *Mata Hari*

You are a beautiful, seductive spy

And so now we come to those

Who are politicians and have left

Such a lasting legacy that their name

Has come to mean something substantial

Synonymous with the heritage they have left

Julius Caesar

Was an extraordinary politician

And leader of warrior conquests and invasions

His name for over two thousand years

Is the origin for the month of July

But his surname gave rise

To terms such as Tsar and Kaiser

And even caesarean

Winston Churchill's personality and character

Was well-defined during World War II

Charismatic, strong, powerful

Almost unwieldy in his stance and policies

The sound of his voice

Being authoritarian and assertive

All those characteristics known as *Churchillian*

Especially, as some try to imitate Winston

Aspiring to ascertain a similar lasting legacy

Margaret Thatcher dominated

British politics throughout the 1980s

Her ideology and policies

Having become known as *Thatcherism*

And those who believe and follow those policies

Are known as *Thatcherites*

You do not even need to have heard those words before

To know exactly what they mean

Tony Blair's political views and ideology

Have become known as *Blairism*

A word that has even entered

The New Penguin Dictionary in 2000

And his followers are known as *Blairites*

Time and history will tell

When another politician

Is so good or bad at what they do

That their name leaves an eternal legacy

Nicknames

Sometimes in life

An off the cuff remark sticks

Becoming an international internet sensation

A new nickname for a politician

That is cemented in history

There is Winston Churchill who became

Synonymous with British Bulldog

Margaret Thatcher the Milk Snatcher

The Grey man, John Major

The *Weapons of Mass Destruction*

Leading to the Iraq War and the nickname, *Bliar, Bliar*

Gordon Brown becoming the Squatter at Number Ten

Dodgy Dave for David Cameron

Theresa Maybe who became *LINO; Leader in name only*

It will be interesting to see

Which of the current politicians

Rise to be given nickname accolades

That go viral and survive in history

Perhaps Piranha Patel

Dominic Raab trying to be suave

Kier Starmer might be sharper but is no charmer

Matt Hancock is just a c…

And I think we'll leave it there

Keep Dancing

Politics is like a dance

There are twists and turns

Rise and fall

Drama

Flecks and bounce

Tension and taut glances

Yet their actual ability to dance

Is highlighted in the phenomenon

That is *Strictly Come Dancing*

Stomping like animals

Graceless and grumpy

Becoming caricature cartoons

Edwina Currie answering back the judges

Jacqui Smith dancing to

'Always Look on the Bright Side of Life'

Ed Balls dancing 'Gangnam Style'

Ann Widdecombe being flung around the floor

All done with humour, enthusiasm and entertainment

Echoing their devotion to politics

Order, Order

It is in the Houses of Parliament

Where behaviour is akin

To that of a jungle

Similar to baboons and monkeys

Chitter-chattering

With booing noises

And "Hear, hear." noises

Rustling sounds of papers

Echoing the rustling sounds

Of apes climbing trees

And when the rowdy animals

Become too excited

With their vocals sounding

Like growls, grunts, hissing and spitting

They are brought back under control

With those famous words,

"Order. Order."

Funeral Song

I want to choose my funeral song

Something appropriate and memorable

It's so easy to choose songs for other people

Elizabeth Taylor and Zsa Zsa Gabor both should have had

'Going to the Chapel and We're Gonna Get Married'

Pity that song didn't exist when Henry VIII was buried

Although 'Eight is the Magic Number' also seems ideal

Of course Nelson Mandela certainly deserves 'Freedom'

Muhammad Ali should have had either

'Eye of the Tiger' or 'We are the Champions'

Donald Trump will obviously want 'I Did it My Way'

And maybe he could pre-record 'Push the Button' just for
  Kim Jung Un

Nigel Farage and Boris Johnson should have 'Rule
  Britannia'

David Attenborough ought to have 'The Lion Sleeps
  Tonight'

In fact he should also have the hymn, 'All Creatures Great
  and Small'

If they ever rebury Elizabeth I she could have 'Like a
  Virgin'

Unlike Hugh Hefner who should've had 'House of the
    Rising Sun'
A totally new meaning of 'Maggie May' for Margaret
    Thatcher
I'm sure all records would have been broken
If The Iron Lady and Arthur Scargill did a duet
'Those Were the Days' and 'Working in a Coal Mine'
    might have been their songs

Jackie Kennedy Onassis would have probably chosen
    'Devil in Disguise' for Marilyn Monroe
Perhaps Hillary Clinton should have 'Stand By Your Man'
Especially after her spat with Tammy Wynette
But back to MY funeral song
'Always Look on the Bright Side of Life' is not loud
enough
I was leaning towards 'Staying Alive'
But in the end I decided to take into consideration where
    I'll end up
Not the original meaning of the song, but hey ho
'Sounds of the Underground'

Timeline

Pre-history/Pre-civilisation (Ancient Greek Myth)

Boreas roams the earth.

10th August 30 BC

Suicide of Cleopatra.

15th March 44 BC

Ides of March.

Assassination of Julius Caesar aged 55.

29th November 1530

Death of Cardinal Wolsey aged 57.

1st October 1553

Coronation of Queen Mary I.

Her reputation for burning Protestants at the stake

earned her the nickname *Bloody Mary*.

12th February 1554

Execution of Lady Jane Grey, the Nine Days'

Queen.

5th November 1605

Gunpowder plot discovered when Guy Fawkes is arrested.

31st January 1606

Death of Guy Fawkes aged 35.

August 1744

Robert Carteret cropped the ears of several horses. He went on to become a Member of Parliament that same year.

1760s

Rumours spread of an illicit affair between the widowed mother of the young King George III, and his tutor John Stuart, 3rd Earl of Bute.

1809

Select Committee in Houses of Commons investigates whether the Duke of York's mistress, Mary Anne Clarke, sold army commissions under his guidance.

1820

Parliament instructed to investigate whether Caroline of Brunswick had committed adultery on her husband George IV.

30th December 1916

Murder of Grigori Rasputin.

17th July 1918

Assassination of the Romanov family, including Anastasia Nikolaevna Romanova aged 17.

4th June 1913 and 6th June 1913

Suffragette Emily Wilding Davison's encounter with King George V's horse, Anmer. She died two days later.

1914

Laurence Housman became a founding member of The United Suffragists. He went on to do many campaigns for the Suffragette movement.

November 1919

Nancy Astor became the first woman to sit as a Member of Parliament.

From 1930 to 1966

Member of Parliament Robert Boothby starts long affair with Lady Dorothy MacMillan, wife of future Prime Minister Harold MacMillan.

1936

Constitutional crisis occurred when Edward VIII wanted to marry Wallis Simpson leading to his abdication.

10th May 1940 to 26th July 1945

Winston Churchill was the UK's wartime Prime Minister.

30th January 1948

Assassination of Mahatma Gandhi aged 78.

1950 to 2001

Tony Benn is Member of Parliament.

9th May 1962

Marilyn Monroe famously sings *Happy Birthday Mr President.*

5th June 1963

John Profumo finally admits he lied to parliament about his affair with Christine Keller.

15th August 1963 to 20th November 1997

Screaming Lord Sutch stands in elections.

22nd November 1963

Assassination of President John F. Kennedy in front of his wife Jaqueline Kennedy.

1964 to 1970, and 1974 to 1976

Harold Wilson is Prime Minister of the United Kingdom.

20th April 1968

Enoch Powell, Member of Parliament for Wolverhampton South West delivers *Rivers of Blood* speech in Birmingham.

1973

Revelation in newspapers of Lord Lambton's threesome with prostitutes and drug taking.

17th November 1973

> President Richard Nixon delivers his famous "I am not a crook" speech.

20th November 1974

> Member of Parliament John Stonehouse fakes his own death.

12th February 1975

> Margaret Thatcher visits Edward Heath after defeating him as Party Leader. He declines her offer and leads to his reputation as the 'Incredible Sulk'.

24th October 1975

> The Thorpe Affair: alleged attempted murder of Norman Scott and death of Rinka the dog.

3rd August 1977

> Heart attack and death of Archbishop Makarios III aged 63.

14th June 1978

> Denis Healy describes Geoffrey Howe as though "being savaged by a dead sheep".

10th January 1979

"Crisis? What Crisis?" interview by Prime Minister James Callaghan on the 1978/1979 Winter of Discontent.

4th May 1979 to 28th November 1990

Margaret Thatcher is the UK's first female Prime Minister.

16th June 1982

Founding of the Official Monster Raving Loony Party.

14th October 1983

Cecil Parkinson resigns after revelation that he had a twelve-year affair with Sara Keays and that Sara was pregnant with his child.

1984

Creation of Lord Buckethead.

1st August 1984

Nancy Reagan prompts Ronald Reagan to say, "doing everything we can."

1984 to 1988

John Major and Edwina Currie have a four-year affair.

1985

Neil Kinnock appoints Peter Mandelson as Director of Communications leading to him being known as a spin doctor, and eventually the nickname 'Prince of Darkness'.

3rd December 1988

Edwina Currie announces that most of Britain's eggs were infected with salmonella.

16th May 1990

John Selwyn Gummer tries to feed his daughter, Cordelia, a beef burger in front of the media during the BSE crisis.

14th November 1990

Michael Heseltine announces his candidacy for leader of Conservative Party to oust Margaret Thatcher.

26th January 1992

Hillary Clinton defends her husband and says, "I'm not sitting here some little woman standing by my man like Tammy Wynette."

27th January 1992

Death of Sally Mugabe, first wife of Robert Mugabe and considered by many as the founding mother of the nation of Zimbabwe.

27th April 1992 to 23rd October 2000

Betty Boothroyd is Speaker of the House.

3rd September 1993

UKIP is founded.

1994-1995, 2001-2006, and 2008-2011

Silvio Berlusconi is Italy's Prime Minister.

1994 to 2010

New Labour branding logo used by the Labour Party.

12th May 1994

Was this the day that the Blair-Brown Deal was agreed?

10th April 1995

The *Guardian* newspaper reports on Jonathan Aitken's dealings in Saudi Arabia, which leads to libel and perjury actions.

August 1996

Marriage of Robert Mugabe and Grace Goreraza, dubbed 'Wedding of the Century' by some of the newspapers in Zimbabwe.

8th May 1997

Introduction of Blair's Babes following the 1997 Labour victory in the General Election.

26th January 1998

President Bill Clinton denies having had "sexual liaisons" with Monica Lewinsky.

17th July 1998

Burial of Anastasia Romanova, 80 years after her assassination.

5th July 2000

Euan Blair gives a false name and old address when found by police inebriated.

16th May 2001

A protestor throws an egg at Labour's Deputy Prime Minister John Prescott who then punches the man.

19th July 2001

Jeffrey Archer found guilty of perjury and sentenced to four-year prison sentence.

11th September 2001

Jo Moore allegedly says in an e-mail when the Twin Towers are attacked and destroyed that it is "…a very good day to get anything out we want to bury. Councillors' expenses?"

2002

Alastair Campbell blasts Andre Suard for defending Cherie Blair; "You're just a fucking hairdresser."

2002

Edwina Currie reveals to the world her four- year affair with John Major in her book, *Currie's Diaries (1987-92)*.

15th March 2005 and 26th March 2005

Deaths of Audrey Callaghan, and eleven days later her husband – the former Prime Minister James Callaghan.

22nd November 2005

Angela Dorothea Merkel becomes The Chancellor of Germany.

12th September 2006

Nigel Farage is elected leader of UKIP for the first time.

9th May 2008

Cherie Blair says that Gordon Brown, in April 2004, tried to drive Tony Blair out of 10 Downing Street by "rattling keys" above his head.

21st May 2009

The *Daily Telegraph* reported on a £30,000 expenses scandal of MP Peter Viggers, which included the infamous Duck House.

5th June 2009

Jacqui Smith resigns following the expenses scandal.

28th April 2010

Gordon Brown refers to Gillian Duffy as a "bigoted woman".

20th November 2010

Anton du Beke and Ann Widdecombe make it to Blackpool week as they dance the Samba with Ann dressed in yellow and being thrown across the dance floor.

19th July 2011

Wendi Deng Murdoch defends her husband by stopping a man about to pie-face her husband, and punches him.

22nd February 2012

MP Eric Joyce is arrested by police on suspicion of attacking up to six politicians.

5th February 2013

Chris Huhne resigns as Member of Parliament after pleading guilty to perverting the course of justice.

April 2013

Iain Duncan Smith declares that you can live on £53.00 per week.

5th December 2013

Death of Nelson Mandela aged 95.

12th September 2014

Death of Ian Paisley aged 88.

18th September 2014

Scottish Referendum of Scottish independence from Great Britain.

October 2014

12 Labours of Vladimir Putin art is released.

4th November 2014

Justin Trudeau becomes Prime Minister in Canada.

20th September 2015

Daily Mail publishes extracts from forthcoming book, *Call Me Dave,* which leads to Piggate.

12th January 2016

Mary Wilson becomes the first spouse of a British Prime Minister to reach the age of 100.

11th April 2016

Dennis Skinner refers to David Cameron as *Dodgy Dave.*

23rd June 2016

Great Britain has EU referendum.

9th July 2016

The *Times* publishes interview with Andrea Leadsom and infamous *motherhood* comments.

12th November 2016

Ed Balls dances 'Gangnam Style' on Strictly Come Dancing.

26th February 2017 to 6th November 2019

Kenneth Clarke, *The Big Beast of British Politics* becomes *Father of the House.*

March 2017

Ruth Davidson tells Nicola Sturgeon to "sit down."

2nd April 2018

Death of Winnie Mandela.

6th August 2018

Boris Johnson's comments in his newspaper column that women who wear the burka look like letterboxes causes outrage and allegedly a rise in Islamophobic attacks.

3rd October 2018

Theresa May dances to *Dancing Queen* at Conservative Party Conference.

14th December 2018

Bronze statue of Emmeline Pankhurst erected to celebrate 100 years since women, aged 30, first got the right to vote.

4th September 2019

Boris Johnson refers to Jeremy Corbyn as a "chlorinated chicken".

6th September 2019

Death of Robert Mugabe aged 95.

10th November 2019

Keith Vaz announces he is retiring from Parliament.

18th November 2019

Good Morning Britain interviews Jennifer Acuri where she clashes with Piers Morgan and Lorraine Kelly over her relationship with Boris Johnson.

11ᵗʰ December 2019

Boris Johnson hides in a fridge to avoid an interview by *Good Morning Britain* presenter.

12ᵗʰ April 2020

Dominic Cummings drives his wife and son to Barnard Castle to test his eyesight.

7ᵗʰ July 2020

Rudy Giuliani reports to the police the incident which is included in the second Borat film.

December 2020

Edited clip of Handforth Parish Council zoom meeting goes viral.

13ᵗʰ February 2021

Donald Trump is acquitted by the Senate on his second impeachment – the charge being incitement of insurrection.

May 2021

Revelation to the public on how Martin Bashir really obtained the interview with Princess Diana 25 years earlier.

More Books By Mario

Birth Life Burial

This is a poetry book concerning birth, life and death and all the ups and downs our unique adventure brings. There are over 100 poems written in a variety of voices and moods. Poems which are endearing and emotive, some that are humorous and comedic, and others which are thought provoking. Spanning a number of topics including childhood, love, parenthood, betrayal, older age, suicide, and death, these memorable and refreshing poems are varied in form (such as rhyme and free verse) and also in length.

There is also a number of allegory poems. The various poems are presented from different perspectives, such as from the parent or the child, the person proposing, the person being cheated upon, and from an independent/third party point of view. Whatever stage of life you may have reached, you will have experienced some of the emotions or events shared in Birth, Life, Burial.

Buy your copy here: <u>https://amzn.to/31oafSt</u>

Myths and Make-Believe

This is a poetry book concerning myths, legends, fairy tales, and other make-believe characters and fictional entities. There are over 100 poems. Examples of Greek Myth characters includes Zeus and Hera, Atlas, Medusa and the Gorgon sisters, Python, Arachne, the Minotaur and the Labyrinth, the Sphynx, the Kraken, and many more.

There is Audhumbla from Norse mythology. From the Old Testament there are poems about Noah, Lot's wife, Cain from Cain and Able, Lilith, David and Goliath, Salome, Angels, and the Devil. Poems about Legends includes King Arthur, Excalibur, and the Lady of the Lake. There are also poems about Dragons, Fairy Tales, Easter Island, Witches, Black Cats, Monsters, Clowns, Ghosts, Werewolves, and the Tooth Fairy. Finally, there are also poems about places such as Ireland, Prague, Cannock Chase, and castles.

The poems are in a variety of voices, and different moods such as serious, thought-provoking and emotive, or humorous and comedic.

Buy your copy here: https://amzn.to/2VPyLef

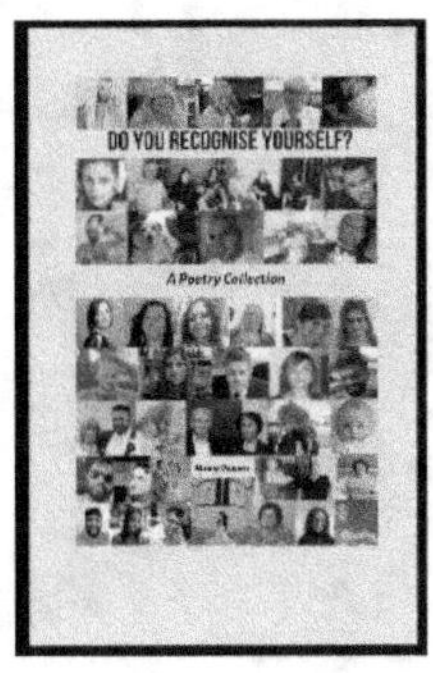

Do You Recognise Yourself?

A colourful, eclectic poetry collection which takes a beautiful, brutally honest and hilarious look at the patchwork of life. Using creative flair and first-rate storytelling skills the author expertly reflects on the weird and wonderful traits of people – both fictitious and real – celebrating the humorous with the irresistible and outing the darker personalities who live and work beside us all.

The author's superb observations of the human psyche, inter-faith relationships, family, writing groups, broken marriages, Brexit, womanisers, anxiety, and even a Wolverhampton Witch are perceptive, thoroughly entertaining and will have you nodding, smiling, empathising and reflecting from beginning to end.

Events, people and situations are embellished, merged and distorted to create a kaleidoscope of rhyme and verse that will resonate with readers from all walks of life. Who knows, you might even recognise yourself in there too.

Buy your copy here: https://amzn.to/3cmAsGM

Animal in You?

Mother Nature is amazing, isn't she? Her animal kingdom is filled with the weirdest and most wonderful creatures in our seas, skies and lands. But have you ever reflected on how deeply the connection between animals and humans runs? And how many fascinating characteristics we have in common? Once this thought's planted in your head, you won't be able to stop thinking about it.

Do you know what animal characteristics you possess?
- Are you the hunter or the prey?
- A lounge lizard or a hard-working ant?
- A beautiful bird of paradise or more like the Tamworth Two? Or an untameable shrew?

Whether the cat's got your tongue or you're in the dog house, or you're wondering how to take care of your human pets, you'll find something funny, irresistible and moving in this fantastic poetry collection.

Buy your copy here: https://amzn.to/3mcnxMd

Glimpses of Epic Greek Myths

This is a poetry book concerning myths, legends, fairy tales, and other make-believe characters and fictional entities. There are over 100 poems. Examples of Greek Myth characters includes Zeus and Hera, Atlas, Medusa and the Gorgon sisters, Python, Arachne, the Minotaur and the Labyrinth, the Sphynx, the Kraken, and many more. There is Audhumbla from Norse mythology. From the Old Testament there are poems about Noah, Lot's wife, Cain from Cain and Able, Lilith, David and Goliath, Salome, Angels, and the Devil. Poems about Legends includes King Arthur, Excalibur, and the Lady of the Lake. There are also poems about Dragons, Fairy Tales, Easter Island, Witches, Black Cats, Monsters, Clowns, Ghosts, Werewolves, and the Tooth Fairy. Finally, there are also poems about places such as Ireland, Prague, Cannock Chase, and castles. The poems are in a variety of voices, and different moods such as serious, thought-provoking and emotive, or humorous and comedic.

Buy your copy here: https://amzn.to/3mlNdGw

What Drink Are You?

What do the beverages that you drink
actually reveal about your personality?
Do you drink tea and/or coffee?
Perhaps a vodka or martini?
Are you hip and trendy with a gin?
Or maybe just a beer drinker?
This is a hilarious take
On your characteristics
Just based on what you drink
Over 100 poems.
Including allegory poems.
Find out if you are
Boring and dull
Or sexy, hot and desirable

After reading this collection
Will you stick to your usual drink?
Or will you change your drink?
Hoping for a brand new and invigorating image.

Buy your copy here: https://amzn.to/3vY5D5B

About the Author

Mario Panayi was born in the UK, but visited his relatives in Cyprus every year during his childhood. It was a very different Cyprus in the 1970s and early 1980s compared to now as Cyprus had been invaded in 1974. The visits he made to Cyprus were very influential on Mario, as he witnessed the aftermath of war such as refugees living in tiny accommodation, running water half a day per week which had to be stored for the whole week, no telephones, and of course more than 2,000 people had disappeared, presumed dead. This included two of his cousins.

It made Mario very conscious of how fortunate most people are in life, including himself, and how precious life is. He also forged a close relationship to his relatives in Cyprus. Mario found that being told he couldn't do things just made him more determined to be able to do things. At school a teacher refused to sign off his university application, explaining that there was no point applying to University because he was not capable academically of getting a degree and would probably not be accepted at University. He applied regardless and got two honours degrees, one postgraduate degree and two Masters degrees, including an MBA.

At a previous job he was told by his manager that he could not write. It was at that point he went on to get his final degree which was a BA (HONS) Philosophy and Creative and Professional Writing, but he never studied poetry.

Mario has found that walking and writing is cathartic and therapeutic.

To date he has published seven poetry books:

- *Birth, Life, Burial* (2018)
- *Myths and Make-Believe* (2018)
- *Do You Recognise Yourself* (2019)
- *Animal in YOU?* (2020)
- *Glimpses of Epic Greek Myths* (2020)
- *What Drink Are You?* (2020)
- *Political Perspectives* (2021)